THE GILE

LINCOLNSHIRE'S
Heritage

LINCOLNSHIRE'S
Heritage

DAVID START & COLLETTE HALL

Photography principally by
Philip Crome

First published 1996
Photographs copyright © 1996 Heritage Lincolnshire
Text copyright © David Start and Collette Hall
First published in the United Kingdom 1996 by
Heritage Lincolnshire
The Old School, Cameron Street, Heckington, Sleaford,
Lincolnshire, NG34 9RW

British Library Cataloguing-in-Publication Data
A CIP catalogue record for this book
is available from the British Library

ISBN 0-948639-16-4

Designed by The S S Crome, Alford, Lincolnshire
Production by Nicholas Russell, Cambridge
Printed in the UK by Balding & Mansell, Kettering

CONTENTS

———— FOREWORD ————

by the Chairman of Heritage Lincolnshire, Dr Michael Ashton

In 1993 Heritage Lincolnshire published *Lincolnshire from the Air* – the Trust's first venture into the realms of popular publishing. The book was a great success and is still selling extremely well. It remains one of the best illustrated guides to Lincolnshire's landscape and heritage. Now in response to many requests the Trust has produced **Lincolnshire's Heritage**, a companion volume to *Lincolnshire from the Air*, which aims to present some of the best of Lincolnshire's historic treasures in a journey through time from the prehistoric period to the modern day. The beautiful photographs and informative text illustrate how our quiet rural county has played a leading role in the development of the English nation. Across the varied landscape of Lincolnshire, in the towns and villages (and sometimes quite unexpectedly in the open countryside) a wide range of ancient ruins and historic buildings bears witness to a colourful and prosperous past. It is, therefore, entirely appropriate that Heritage Lincolnshire, an independent charitable trust established to protect and promote the heritage of the county for the benefit of Lincolnshire people and of visitors, should produce this book. I am sure that it will reveal some fascinating aspects of historic Lincolnshire to seasoned yellow–bellies and visitors alike.

Michael Ashton

ACKNOWLEDGEMENTS

Lincolnshire's Heritage must surely be a most appropriate title to be published by Heritage Lincolnshire. The Trust, which was set up by Lincolnshire County Council in 1988 with a brief to promote Lincolnshire's Heritage in its widest aspects, is still supported by the County Council with a generous annual grant. None of the work of the Trust would be possible without the continuing support of the County Council. Heritage Lincolnshire is an independent charitable trust receiving funding from a wide variety of other sources including District Councils, charitable trusts, local and national heritage bodies, commercial sponsorship and private donations, all of which play their part in ensuring the future of Lincolnshire's heritage and the Heritage Trust.

Lincolnshire's Heritage is the product of the knowledge and good–will of many people and we are indebted to all those who have given so freely of their time and expertise. Many of the photographs were taken by Philip Crome and we owe much to his skill and perseverance. Photographs in the book that do not bear specific credits were taken by Philip Crome or the authors. A full list of photographic credits is given on page 123. Thanks are due to the staff of City and County Museum, the Social and Economic Development Unit of Lincolnshire County Council, the British Museum, Scunthorpe Museum and Sheffield Museum for their assistance in locating and obtaining photographs. Other photographs have been supplied by Ashley Black, Chris Cruickshank, Ian George, Hilary Healey, David Stocker and David Vale.

Once again, the design and layout of the book have been expertly handled by Sarah Crome and the project management and co–ordination by Philip Crome (when he wasn't taking photographs!) For technical assistance we are indebted to Nicholas Russell.

We have received much assistance and advice with the production of captions. Thanks for help and information go to Geoff Barry (PR Consultant, Fantasy Island), Mark Bennet (Lincolnshire County Council), Tony Black, Philip Crome, Julia Dabbs (Lincolnshire Library Service), Andrew Davies (Museum of Lincolnshire Life), Julie Duxbury (Lincoln City Council), The Environment Agency, Terry Hancock, Hilary Healey, Linda Hill, John Honnor (Welland & Deepings IDB), Eric Iredale, Mick Jones (City of Lincoln Archaeology Unit), Andrew Keeling (East Midlands Tourist Board), Chris Lester, Paul Naylor (Anglian Water), Margaret Nieke (English Heritage), Powergen staff at Cottam Power Station, James Rackham, John Redshaw (Lincolnshire Trust for Nature Conservation), David Robinson, Stewart Squires (Newark and Sherwood District Council), Maria Vincent (East Lindsey Tourism Dept.), Arthur Ward (Lincoln City Council) and Neil Wright.

Sarah Willis, the Trust's Administrator, and her assistant Sally Dawkins, helped compile the subscriber sponsor lists and dealt with the copious amount of paperwork generated in the process. All of the Trust's staff advised, prompted, argued, discussed and generally helped with the text. Particular thanks go to Tom Lane for his advice on matters prehistoric.

Once again we are grateful to Ruth Moore who has patiently edited the texts, corrected the worst excesses of our grammar and punctuation and generally tried to achieve consistency between two very different authors. For any omissions and errors that remain, we take full responsibility.

Finally, on a more personal level, we would both like to thank our respective partners, Ruth Moore and Ashley Black, for their patience, support and forbearance during the long and often disruptive process of producing this book.

David Start and Collette Hall
Heritage Lincolnshire
July, 1996

INTRODUCTION

Many people, from inside and outside Lincolnshire, enjoyed *Lincolnshire from the Air* and we have often been asked to produce another volume ... here is that companion volume – **Lincolnshire's Heritage**. However, this is not another book of aerial photographs (although a few are included here) but a celebration of the landscapes, monuments and buildings that combine to create Lincolnshire's heritage.

The idea behind this book started out quite simply ... choose the best in Lincolnshire's heritage throughout the ages, take photographs, and put the whole lot together for our readers to enjoy from their armchairs – or to go out and visit. The reality was quite different. As with *Lincolnshire from the Air*, the more we looked and the more we photographed, the more we realised just how much we would have to leave out. The county is so rich in historic buildings and ancient sites that this book could be three times the size and still fail to cover the wonderful variety of historic treasures in Lincolnshire. You will find here much that is familiar but we hope that some of the subjects will be new to you and that you will enjoy the same sense of discovery that we experienced while compiling these pages. In response to many requests, *all* the photographs in **Lincolnshire's Heritage** are in colour and the accompanying texts are brief but, we hope, interesting and informative. Our intention was that everything in this book should be on public view or open to visitors and that is largely true although just a few of the objects described here may now be out of the county (some in the British Museum).

In **Lincolnshire's Heritage** we have not tried to write a history book. There are many excellent and scholarly works on the history of Lincolnshire and we have included a reading list for those who wish to pursue further studies in the archaeology and buildings of Lincolnshire. We have tried to capture the essence of Lincolnshire by exploring the elements which combine to make up the distinctive character of the county. In order to produce the texts which follow, we have relied heavily on the existing books about Lincolnshire, and on the knowledge and expertise of many local specialists. We would particularly recommend the Lincolnshire volume of *The Buildings of England* by Pevsner, Harris and Antram, and the

volumes in the History of Lincolnshire series, published by the Society for Lincolnshire History and Archaeology.

The best known image of Lincolnshire is that of its fenland landscape of wide flat fields, enormous skies and intensive agriculture. The reality of Lincolnshire, as its inhabitants know well, is one of diverse landscapes and subtle regional variations that blend to form a county that cannot easily be characterised. The historic county of Lincolnshire extended from the Humber to the Wash and was the second largest in the land at 2791 square miles. The local government changes of 1974 carved off over 500 square miles into Humberside but, as of April 1996, Lincolnshire is once again re–united, if only in name, with the creation of the independent local authorities of North, and North East Lincolnshire. In this book, as in *Lincolnshire from the Air*, we have disregarded modern alterations and included all of the historic county.

Our journey through Lincolnshire's heritage begins about 10,000 years ago with the resettlement of the region in the wake of the last ice age, although there is no doubt that there was a human presence here before and between the various ice ages. Stone axe–heads made over 150,000 years ago have been found in several places (notably at Kirmington) but they lie in gravel deposits laid down when the Lincolnshire landscape was being shaped by ice, lakes and fast flowing rivers. No–one can tell where these ancient artefacts originated or what type of landscape was inhabited by their makers.

Evidence of prehistoric Lincolnshire remains slight although our knowledge is growing all the time. It is clear that the region was as populous as many of those which boast impressive prehistoric stone circles and chambered tombs, but such features are neither favoured by our geology, nor by the centuries of intensive agriculture which has swept away so much of our past. During Roman times Lincoln was elevated from a native settlement, first to a fortress and then to a city; a status which endured through Anglo–Saxon and Viking times and which set the stage for its eminence during the medieval period. There are several unique survivals from these times and there can be few books on early medieval architecture which fail to cite the Jews House in Lincoln and the manor house at Boothby Pagnell as among the best examples in the land. The wealth and splendour of the medieval county can be seen also in the many fine 14th and 15th century churches, whose spires still pierce the fenland skies or stand, squat towered, in the valleys of the Wolds.

In the centuries that follow, fine architecture remains a feature of town and countryside and examples can be found around the county which illustrate the way building styles changed with new fashions and improved technology. Tudor tower houses and Elizabethan country homes display inventive use of brick, then a comparatively new building material, whilst the elegant Georgian terraces in our county towns show a new concentration on simplicity and proportion. The Victorian age was one of invention and industry, when the county was criss–crossed by railways and dotted with monumental industrial buildings, such as the Bass Maltings at Sleaford. The legacy of the 20th century will include structures ranging from motorways and airfields to the new

Lincolnshire University, all of which will add to the county's rich heritage for future generations.

The organisation of the book is broadly chronological. The 8000 years from the middle stone age (mesolithic) to the coming of the Romans is grouped together under *The Ancient Landscape* (with apologies to prehistorians). The design of succeeding chapters owes much to the current school curriculum and the periods loosely conform to the structure presently in use in schools. The time–line shown below gives the periods covered by the chapters.

We hope that this book will encourage people to understand and enjoy Lincolnshire's rich heritage. The work of the Trust, as the county's leading heritage organisation, is to promote, protect and preserve the historic remains of our past and to help Lincolnshire people, and our visitors, appreciate and treasure this great county.

A SLICE THROUGH TIME

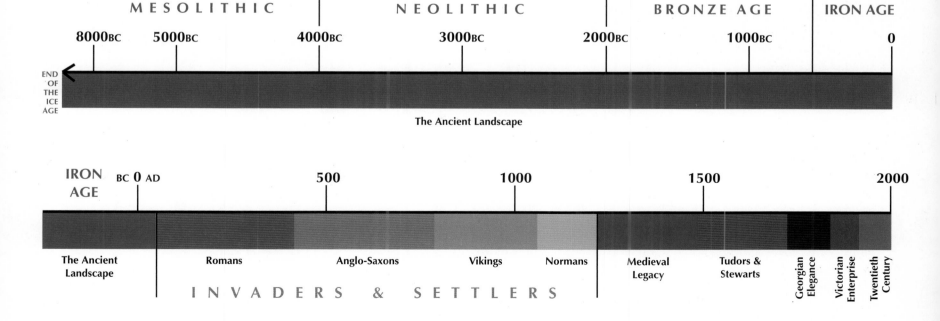

MESOLITHIC		NEOLITHIC		BRONZE AGE	IRON AGE
8000BC 5000BC	4000BC	3000BC	2000BC	1000BC	0

END OF THE ICE AGE

The Ancient Landscape

IRON AGE	BC 0 AD	500	1000	1500	2000

| The Ancient Landscape | Romans | Anglo-Saxons | Vikings | Normans | Medieval Legacy | Tudors & Stewarts | Georgian Elegance | Victorian Enterprise | Twentieth Century |

INVADERS & SETTLERS

THE ANCIENT LANDSCAPE

Artist's impression of the Iron Age settlement at Brayford Pool. Dating from the 1st century BC, it was the predecessor of Roman Lindum and the city of Lincoln.

LCC, Archaeology Collection.

Our story of Lincolnshire begins about 10,000 years ago at the end of the last Ice Age. As the vegetation recovered and wild animals returned, nomadic groups of hunters and gatherers began to visit the county, setting up temporary camps and making clearings in the new woodland. They worked flints for the blades of their tools and weapons and these are often all that remains to testify to their presence.

Hunting evolved into farming about 6000 years ago bringing a more settled lifestyle and heralding such innovations as the use of pottery and the building of burial mounds (barrows) and other ritual monuments. Few settlements from this time are known but the distribution of archaeological objects suggests that the county was extensively populated. Trading in raw materials, notably hard stone for making axe–heads, took place and a pattern of ancient trackways developed reaching throughout the county and beyond. From around 4000 years ago, stone tools were gradually replaced by the use of bronze and the earliest 'villages' began to form. The villages grew as the economy developed and social distinctions of rich and poor are noticeable. By 2500 years ago the working of iron had been discovered and great skill is demonstrated in the production of prestigious objects, often weapons. Social organisation was tribal by this time and there was a well developed network of villages and larger centres many of which formed the basis of towns that flourished in Roman times.

THE SUBMERGED FOREST

The Lincolnshire coastline was not always as it is today. Ten thousand years ago, at the end of the last Ice Age, the North Sea was dry land. As the climate gradually warmed up a forest grew, way out into what is now the sea. It probably began as a pine forest but by about 7000 years ago it had developed into a mixed forest with alder, lime, hazel, oak and birch. As the water level slowly rose, the forest floor became damp and then waterlogged and a blanket of peat formed around the trees. Eventually, the wet conditions killed the trees and they fell, leaving a jumble of stumps and trunks half buried by peat. By about 3000 years ago the sea had covered the stumps, burying them beneath a layer of marine sediment. In more recent times coastal erosion between Mablethorpe and Ingoldmells has cut into the buried layers exposing this submerged forest.

10,000 years ago dry land joined Britain and Europe and the coastline was very different from that of today.

The ancient tree stumps of the submerged forest appear off the coast near Anderby Creek at low tide. The layer of peat that engulfed and killed the trees, complete with remains of the tree roots, survives in some places.

LINCOLNSHIRE'S EARLIEST INHABITANTS

Whether anyone lived in Lincolnshire before or between the Ice Ages, we cannot tell. The earliest Lincolnshire inhabitants we know about came to this region after the last Ice Age, 9000 – 10,000 years ago. By then, the arctic conditions had given way to forests of oak, elm, birch and lime. Deer, wild ox (aurochs) and wild boar flourished in this new environment, attracting groups of nomadic hunters and gatherers who probably set up temporary, seasonal camps. Evidence of their presence is plentiful but is limited to their distinctive flint artefacts which still survive in the soil. Their way of life changed little in 3000 years, until the introduction of farming techniques, around 6000 years ago. Traces of these stone age (or mesolithic) hunters have been discovered in several parts of the county, usually on the uplands: notably north east of Scunthorpe, in the Grantham and Ancaster areas and at Hall Hill on the southern edge of the Wolds.

West Keal on Hall Hill at the southern extreme of the Wolds. The light sandy soils on this steep scarp overlooking the Fens must have been an attractive proposition to early settlers.

THE FIRST VILLAGES

About 6000 years ago the change to farming and a more settled way of life had begun. Domesticated sheep, pigs and cattle were reared and primitive forms of barley, wheat and beans were grown. Hunting and gathering still provided some of the diet, and flint arrowheads are a common find on Lincolnshire's fields.

Flint arrowheads are a common find on Lincolnshire's fields. This collection from Ropsley and Humby includes Neolithic leaf–shaped, and Bronze Age barbed and tanged, arrowheads.

Dwellings became more permanent and substantial, and groups of houses (the first villages) began to appear. The evidence for these early settlements is slight and few have been discovered. Often the only trace left is a horseshoe shaped ditch (known as an eaves–drip gully) which was dug around the circular huts to prevent rainwater running across the floor. Occasionally remnants of the hearth or the posts that supported the roof may be found, but these remains are so fragile they rarely survive modern intensive farming techniques.

An excavation at Deeping St. James located a series of inter–cutting circular ditches which indicate a succession of late Neolithic and Early Bronze Age round houses.

BARROWS

A barrow is a mound of earth covering graves. Barrows are usually encircled by ditches from which the mound material was dug. The Neolithic farmers who settled here about 6000 years ago built long barrows – long banks of earth which were communal burial places, the bones of the dead being piled into a chamber or onto a floor which was later covered by the mound. In the Bronze Age, (4000 – 2500 years ago) smaller, round barrows were built. They usually covered just one or two graves, although other burials were often added in the sides of the mound. The remains are either skeletons or cremations in urns, often accompanied by offerings of pottery, tools and jewellery.

Barrows usually occur in groups and are often built on the skyline or in prominent places. It is thought that these barrow cemeteries may have marked tribal territories. There are hundreds of barrows in Lincolnshire, although few now survive as mounds owing to many centuries of ploughing and levelling.

An 'incense cup' from a Bronze Age barrow at Dowsby, near Bourne.

Bronze Age round barrow at Burgh Top, near Ludford.

On Bully Hill, near Tathwell, six of a group of seven Bronze Age barrows cluster together on the skyline to form one of the most conspicuous barrow cemeteries in Lincolnshire. Clearly their builders intended the barrows to be seen, perhaps to proclaim their territory or maybe to venerate the spirits of the dead. At sunrise and sunset, the barrows appear in sharp silhouette to west or east and Bully Hill takes on a timeless and mysterious appearance.

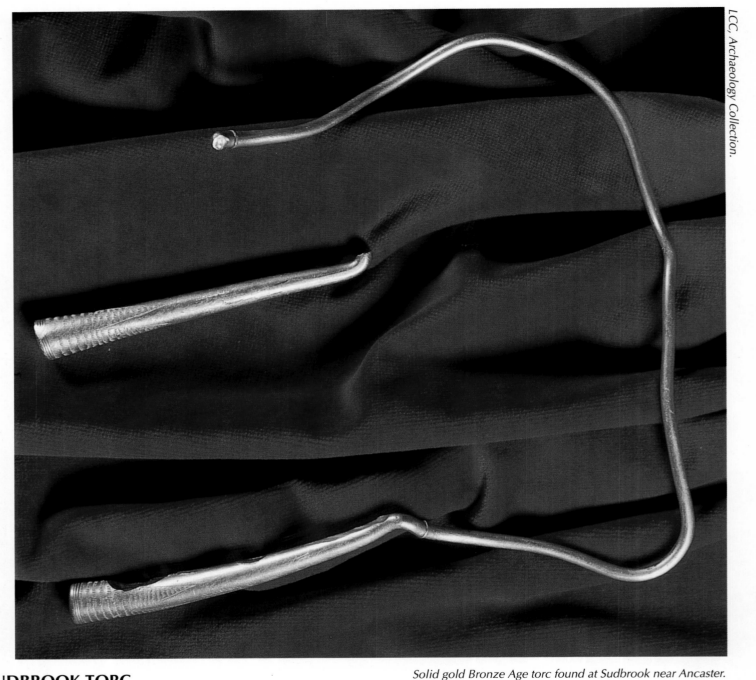

Solid gold Bronze Age torc found at Sudbrook near Ancaster.

THE SUDBROOK TORC

This beautiful object is a solid gold neck ring or torc thought to have been made in the Late Bronze Age, about 3000 years ago. It was found in 1992 by Royce Marshal while he was harrowing a field at Sudbrook, near Ancaster. This torc is one of only seven examples of its type known and the first to be found in Britain. There are only two other known pieces of Bronze Age goldwork from Lincolnshire: a twisted wire torc from Haxey (now in the British Museum) and, from Cuxwold, a massive gold armlet which has not been seen since the 18th century. Torcs were a symbol of power and wealth during the Bronze Age and this find is particularly important as it gives some insight into the development of social status.

THE ANCIENT ROADS OF LINCOLNSHIRE

From prehistoric times the uplands of Lincolnshire have provided a series of route–ways for trade and travel. The limestone ridge known as Lincoln Edge or Cliff is part of the course of a main route, the Jurassic Way, which runs north–south through Lincolnshire to join the hills which carry it southwards to the Cotswolds and the Mendips. North of Lincoln this road was later known as Pottergate – an indication of the merchandise it carried. Other ancient route–ways are known, all clinging to the high ground and giving access to the early settlements and the Fen edge. Mareham Lane followed the eastern edge of the limestone ridge; Sewstern Lane ran from East Anglia to the Trent near Newark; Salters Way linked the coast (and its saltpans) to the Midlands. High Street passed along the western edge of the Wolds with Barton Street on the eastern side. Linking the roads across the southern Wolds is the Bluestone Heath Road – still a wonderfully timeless and evocative road today. When these trackways were established cannot be stated with any certainty, but it is likely they were in use before the Romans came; some were redeveloped as Roman roads and most may still be travelled today.

The Bluestone Heath Road offers some of the best views of the Lincolnshire Wolds as it meanders from Welton le Wold to Driby Top.

ANCIENT POTTERY

The development and use of pottery marks an important stage in the growth of technology. The earliest pottery found in Lincolnshire was made about 5500 years ago at about the time when farming and a more settled lifestyle began. The first pots, which were round–bottomed and undecorated, were made by coiling thin strips of clay into the required shape, smoothing over the joins, and 'firing' on an open fire. As methods improved, flat bottoms and distinctive decorations were introduced. The designs, which were made by stamping or cutting geometric patterns on the pots before they were fired, give us a rare glimpse of prehistoric art. Ancient pottery is very fragile and whole pots rarely survive. Those that we have were found in graves under barrows where they were placed with offerings of food and drink for the dead, or were used to contain cremated ashes. The design of Lincolnshire's prehistoric pottery reflects styles throughout the rest of England and is evidence of widespread cultural contact.

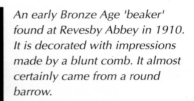

An early Bronze Age 'beaker' found at Revesby Abbey in 1910. It is decorated with impressions made by a blunt comb. It almost certainly came from a round barrow.

LCC, Archaeology Collection.

An early Bronze Age 'collared urn' found in 1870 in a field known as 'The Round Hills' (probably barrows) at Dunston.

LCC, Archaeology Collection.

18

The fort at Honington Camp, near Grantham. A public footpath skirts the eastern edge of the fort but does not give access to the interior.

IRON AGE FORTS

About 3000 years ago a distinctive new form of settlement began to appear in southern England and Wales. Forts were built, defended by earthen ramparts, sometimes with walls of timber or stone added, and encircled by deep ditches. They were usually sited to take advantage of natural defensive features such as hills, promontories and cliffs. Few were built in eastern England where the landscape rarely offered the opportunities for defended hilltops. Lincolnshire's best example is Honington Camp, near Grantham. There are smaller forts at Round Hills near Ingoldsby, Careby Camp near Bourne and Yarborough Camp near Croxton. Defended forts of this type often contain archaeological evidence of Iron Age occupation and appear to have been settlements rather than emergency strongholds. They were built and used throughout the Iron Age and into Roman times.

THE WITHAM SHIELD

This remarkable shield, one of the finest of its type in Europe, was dredged from the River Witham near Lincoln in 1826. Although made of bronze, it is thought to be Iron Age; the elaborate artwork (known as La Tène style) belonging to the period around 250 BC. The shield is formed from two long pieces of beaten sheet bronze only 0.3mm thick which would originally have been fastened to a wooden or leather backing. Masking the join is a raised spine with three bosses which are decorated with superb incised and relief Celtic designs with pieces of coral set in the central boss. A stylised boar was mounted across the centre of the shield, although only the rivet holes now survive.

The Witham Shield is far too delicate ever to have withstood the blow of a sword and is unlikely to have been for use in warfare. It was more likely to have been a symbol of wealth and status of a chieftain or nobleman. Perhaps it was given as an offering to a river or water god, or accompanied a dead chieftain on his final journey down the river? The shield is on permanent display at the British Museum and there is a copy in the City and County Museum at Lincoln.

The Witham Shield, a masterpiece of Iron Age art and metalwork, was found in the River Witham, near Lincoln, in 1826.

British Museum.

INVADERS & SETTLERS

LCC, Archaeology Collection.

Roman sculpture of a boy charioteer, probably from a tombstone, found in Lincoln.

Lincolnshire, like other eastern coastal counties, has been in the forefront of 'invasions' from Europe throughout its history. During the years 43 – 1066, a succession of peoples arrived in this region, attracted by Lincolnshire's fertile soils and gentle landscape. Some invasions were politically motivated and achieved by military force, others were periods of steady colonisation over decades by land seekers from Europe and Scandinavia. In 43 a Roman army 40,000 strong arrived in Britain and imposed a completely new political and material structure on the country. For nearly 400 years Lincolnshire people appear to have adapted readily to the Roman way of life. Dismay and fear surely followed when administration and protection were withdrawn from Britain by an ailing Roman Empire in 410. In the wake of the Romans followed a long period of colonisation by Scandinavian and Germanic settlers (the Anglo–Saxons) when England, the land of the Angles, was born. By the late 8th century there were new and dangerous visitors, the Vikings who came first as raiders but stayed as settlers and farmers.

Throughout these times, the struggle for the sovereignty of England continued. It reached a turning point in 1066 when William of Normandy, convinced of his right to the English throne, conquered England with an army of fewer than 10,000 men following his famous victory at the Battle of Hastings.

THE ROMANS
AD 43 – 410

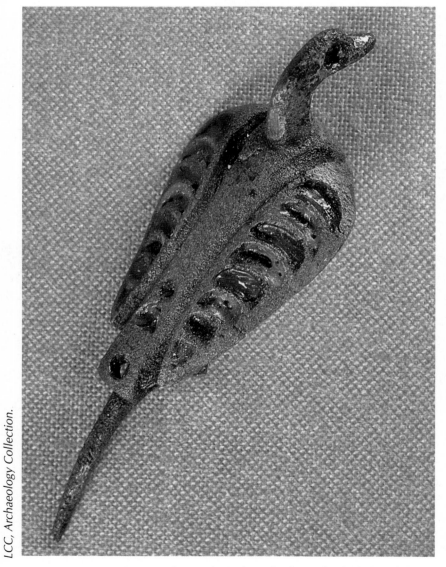

LCC, Archaeology Collection.

A Roman bronze brooch, in the form of a duck, found during the excavation of the Roman aqueduct in Lincoln in 1952.

In the year 43, a Roman army of 40,000 landed in Kent and began the invasion of Britain. One legion (4800 soldiers) was dispatched to the Lincolnshire area and quickly established the northern part of a frontier zone which reached from the Humber to Exeter. They built a frontier road along the line of Ermine Street and the Fosse Way (now the A15 and A46) and established a chain of small forts along it. For a while, Lincolnshire was part of the frontier zone and by 61, a legionary fortress had been built at Lincoln. The Romans would have been content to go no further, but rebellion in Wales and Yorkshire caused the armies to march north and by 71 the legion had built a new base at York and Lincoln's strategic importance dwindled. However, further prestige was to follow and by 96 Lincoln had been granted the status of a *colonia* (a settlement for retired soldiers), one of only four in the country. It was known then as *Lindum Colonia*, from which the modern name derives. The town grew in importance throughout the Roman period until the withdrawal of Roman administration around 410.

Beyond Lincoln, the countryside was rapidly 'Romanised' with the establishment of a new road system and a network of small towns. Many of the towns grew from the forts built along the roads and some (as at Horncastle and Caistor) developed into local administrative and market centres. Rural settlement prospered with existing farmsteads rebuilt in stone and new 'villa' style farms established (e.g. at Scampton and Norton Disney).

For nearly 400 years the Romans brought relative peace and unity to lowland Britain with a level of economic stability and administration not seen before in these islands. In the early fifth century they abandoned Britain, withdrawing military and governmental control but leaving a legacy of planned roads and towns many of which endure to this day.

David Vale.

NEWPORT ARCH

The gates of Roman Lincoln are justly famous and Newport Arch is the most impressive and substantial remnant of any surviving Roman town gateway in Britain. The first gateway on this site served the fortress and would have been built of timber with earth ramparts on either side. When Lincoln became a *colonia*, around the end of the first century, the fortress was dismantled and a major programme of public building was begun. The new walls and gateways were of stone and were purposely grand to emphasise the status of the city and of Roman power.

Today only the inner wall of the Roman north gateway survives. Originally it was a tunnel–like structure with large towers flanking it and probably a guardhouse above; all modified and re–used during medieval times. In 1784 the outer part of the gateway was dismantled and the whole structure was very nearly demolished. Since then, some parts of the arch have collapsed and been repaired, but the worst injury came in 1964 when it was partly demolished by a lorry. Newport Arch today is a careful reconstruction of the original.

Newport Arch in Lincoln is the most impressive and substantial remnant of any surviving Roman town gateway in Britain. Comparison of the photograph with the artist's impression of the original structure shows the rise in ground level since the gate was built.

THE MINT WALL

Although several stretches of the defensive wall and remains of four of the gateways of Roman Lincoln are visible today, very little survives above ground of the temples, shops, public buildings and houses which once lay within the town walls. Successive generations of decay, demolition and re–use have removed most of the traces of the Roman structures. Thus it is all the more remarkable that one wall has survived for over 1800 years, relatively unscathed, to a height of about six metres. The Mint Wall, at the rear of Castle Hotel on Westgate, is one of the best surviving examples of the wall of a Roman building in Britain. It is over 20 metres long and one metre wide, built of limestone with tile bonding courses at intervals of about 1.6 metres. It is thought to be part of the rear wall of the Roman *basilica* or town hall, estimated to have been 70 metres long when built. The Mint Wall owes its survival to sturdy construction and its incorporation into a succession of structures over the centuries, as can be seen by the many minor repairs and alterations on its surface.

The Mint Wall in Lincoln is one of the best surviving examples of a wall of a Roman building in Britain. Thought to be the rear wall of the Roman town hall, it is over 20 metres long and 6 metres high.

ROMAN ROADS AND TOWNS

Roman military strategy involved the construction of a well planned road system with forts spaced along the road at distances of a day or half a day's march. In this way the Roman army controlled the countryside and ensured it could reach any part of the province rapidly. However, once the initial campaign to conquer Britain was complete the roads stimulated the growth of trade and many of the forts developed into small towns.

The major Roman route through Lincolnshire was Ermine Street which linked London with the north, coming up to Lincoln and proceeding on to meet the Humber at Winteringham. The Fosse Way met Ermine Street immediately south of Lincoln, continuing south west to Somerset. These, and other major routes, were surfaced with stone but many minor roads and tracks in the county remained unsurfaced.

Lincoln, and several smaller towns, lay on the route of Ermine Street. At Ancaster a fort was established on the site of an existing settlement – a common Roman policy. This fort later developed into a small town which was provided with a town wall in the late 3rd century. The outline of the defences is nearly rectangular with curved corners and Ermine Street (now the B6403) passes through, dividing the town into two unequal portions. In the field opposite the church, grass covered banks now mark the line of the Roman town wall and associated ditch.

Ermine Street (now the B6403) passing through the modern village of Ancaster. The Roman town lies at the far end of the present settlement, including the area around the church and the field opposite.

Stone coffins from the Roman cemetery now in Ancaster churchyard.

*One of the best preserved
sections of the Car Dyke
at Martin. A waymarked
trail follows the Car Dyke
from Potterhanworth
Booths to Martin.*

ROMAN WATERWAYS

The Romans were great civil engineers who built not only a whole new system of roads, forts and towns, but also dug waterways to link river routes and, perhaps, to improve drainage. The Romans probably built the Foss Dyke, a navigable canal still in use today, linking Brayford Pool in Lincoln with the River Trent at Torksey. Another ancient watercourse usually presumed to be Roman is the Car Dyke, which runs 122 km (76 miles) from Lincoln to Waterbeach in Cambridgeshire. For most of its course it was carefully engineered to skirt the Fen edge, joining the rivers Slea, Glen and Welland. Although some sections are now filled in and levelled, others still function as part of the present day drainage system. The original function of the Car Dyke is debatable; it was once thought to be a continuous navigable channel carrying agricultural produce from the Fens to the Roman towns of Lincoln and York. However, archaeological investigations have now shown this to be unlikely and its use as a catchwater drain, or even just a major land boundary, seems more likely.

LCC, Archaeology Collection.

Engraving of a Roman mosaic with dolphins and hearts. The floor was discovered near Exchequergate, Lincoln in 1879. It still survives in a chamber entered by a manhole at the rear of Exchequergate, but there is no public access.

ROMAN MOSAICS

The Romans introduced the techniques of building in stone to Britain, developing extensive planned towns, often with lavish public buildings. The local population were encouraged to adopt the Roman way of life and appear to have been content to do so, constructing stone houses in the towns and countryside. The more affluent among them decorated their houses in Roman style, with mosaic floors composed of many thousands of stone cubes (*tesserae*) set in geometric patterns, some incorporating fish, birds, animals or deities. Such floors have been found in the buried remains of Roman buildings in Lincoln and in the larger Roman farms, often termed villas, in the countryside. Several villas with mosaic floors were discovered in the late 17th and early 18th centuries but sadly, few of them were preserved. Fragments of mosaics are exhibited in the Cathedral cloister and Newark museum, and more substantial remains are on display in Scunthorpe Museum (from Winterton villa) and the British Museum (from Horkstow villa). Local artists, notably William Fowler of Winterton, drew the mosaics when they were discovered; often these drawings form the only surviving record of this remarkable Roman craft.

RITUAL AND RELIGION

Evidence of Roman influence in Lincolnshire is plentiful, particularly in the form of objects, lost or discarded, and now buried in the soil. Inscriptions, statues and reliefs, carved in stone, were a popular form of Roman expression and many survive to give us a fascinating glimpse of the religion and social structure of the time.

The Romans were preoccupied with death and burial customs and introduced the custom of marking graves with tombstones upon which were recorded the details of the deceased. Several such tombstones have been found in Lincoln, among them that of Gaius Valerius, a soldier and standard–bearer of the Ninth Legion. In translation, his inscription reads: *Gaius Valerius, son of Gaius, of the Maecian voting tribe, soldier of the Ninth Legion, standard bearer of the century of Hospes, aged 35, with 14 years service, left instruction in his will for this to be set up. Here he lies.*

Ritual and religion played a central part in the life of the Romano–British and their Celtic predecessors and the new religions of the Romans merged with the native traditions to create a bewildering profusion of deities. The 'mother–goddesses' or *Deae Matres* were a powerful symbol of fertility, usually depicted as three females holding various forms of food. A particularly fine example of the *Deae Matres*, showing three seated, apparently pregnant, women was unearthed during grave–digging at Ancaster in 1831. The sculpture was found close to a small stone altar and is thought to have been in its original position on a shrine.

The tombstone of Gaius Valerius, a Roman soldier and standard–bearer of the Ninth Legion. (Now in City & County Museum, Lincoln)

LCC, Archaeology Collection.

The Deae Matres: three mother–goddesses from Ancaster. A powerful symbol of fertility in Roman times. (Now in Grantham Museum)

LCC, Grantham Museum.

INVADERS & SETTLERS
ANGLO-SAXONS & VIKINGS
410–1066

During the late 4th century groups of Danish and German settlers (the Anglo–Saxons) began to raid and colonise the east coast of Britain. The invasion was a gradual process made possible by the diminishing military power of Rome. In the 4th century Lincolnshire was a prosperous region and a tempting proposition to the incomers. At first some resistance was offered and it is likely that the town walls at Horncastle and Caistor were built in response to the Anglo–Saxon threat but in 410, Rome cut her losses and abandoned Britain, instructing the towns to provide for their own defence. Roman currency and economy collapsed, towns and villas decayed, and Britain reverted to a warrior culture. The Anglo-Saxons settled throughout Lincolnshire, their language and religion intermingling with Celtic and Roman traditions and creating the English nation.

Over the next two centuries a new political structure emerged. By 700 stable Anglo-Saxon kingdoms were established (Lincolnshire forming Lindsey and part of Outer Mercia). Christianity was re–introduced and several monasteries were founded in the county, notably at Bardney, Crowland and Partney. Recent remarkable archaeological discoveries at Flixborough, near Scunthorpe, have revealed an aristocratic settlement of 8th century date with many items of beautiful metalwork, including unprecedented quantities of *styli* used for writing. However, peace was not to last for long – in the late 8th century the Vikings began a succession of seasonal raids on the east coast of England concentrating on religious shrines and monasteries. By 865 as these hit and run raids gave way to an extended campaign for conquest in Yorkshire and East Anglia, Lincolnshire became a war zone. That Vikings settled here is evidenced by the county's numerous village names ending in '–by' and it was from Gainsborough that King Swein of Denmark and his son Cnut mounted their final invasion of England in 1013–16.

LCC, Archaeology Collection.

Anglo–Saxon brooch made of gilded bronze with silver plates on its knobs and corners. It was found at Ruskington in 1975, in the grave of a young woman.

The Elloe Stone, near Moulton, is said to mark the meeting place of the court of the wapentake of Elloe.

THE ELLOE STONE
SAXON TIMES TO INDICATE
HUNDRED OF ELLOE COURTS
COUNCIL BY F DRING ESQ THE
PUBLIC SUBSCRIPTION ON JUNE 22
CORONATION OF KING GEORGE V

St. Guthlac's Cross is the oldest of several boundary stones which marked the limits of the domain of Crowland Abbey.

ANGLO-SAXON STONES

Many fragments of Anglo-Saxon sculpture survive around the county, often incorporated into the fabric of later churches. Two unusual examples, set up as marker stones, are the Elloe Stone and St. Guthlac's Cross. Both may be Anglo-Saxon in origin although their dating is uncertain.

The Elloe Stone lies on the boundary between Moulton and Whaplode parishes. It is the upper part of a wheel-headed cross and, although very weathered, the remains of interlace decoration of the 10th or 11th century can still be discerned. It was found buried early this century and mounted in a block recording its re–erection to celebrate the coronation of George V. It is said to mark the meeting place of the wapentake court of Elloe, the largest wapentake (district) of Holland.

St. Guthlac's Cross is thought to be one of several boundary stones that were erected to mark the limits of the lands of Crowland Abbey following a series of disputes with neighbouring abbeys. About a metre of the cross shaft survives, inscribed in Latin which, translated, reads *This rock, I say, is Guthlac's utmost bound.* Crowland Abbey was founded in 716 by King Ethelbald in honour of St. Guthlac, a soldier and the son of a nobleman, who gave up the military life to become a monk. He chose to live as a hermit in the Fens, landing on the desolate island of Crowland in 699.

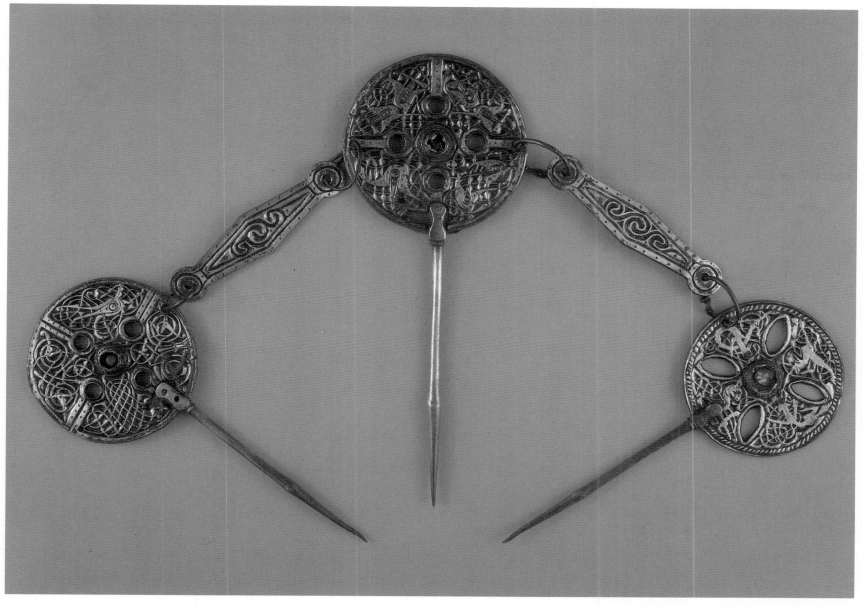

British Museum.

Triple silver pins found in the River Witham in 1826 and now in the British Museum.

SILVER PINS FROM THE RIVER WITHAM

One of the finest pieces of Anglo-Saxon jewellery in the country was found at Fiskerton when the River Witham was being deepened in 1826. It is a complete linked triple pin set made of gilded silver, originally with glass settings at the centres of each pin. The right hand pin is a replacement and is slightly different to the other two. All have elaborate carvings of exotic animals surrounded by interlaced design typical of the second half of the 8th century. The pins, which must have belonged to someone of considerable wealth and status, would have been used as a showy dress or cloak fastening. Single pins and fragments from linked sets survive elsewhere but no other complete set is known in the country. The Witham pins were acquired by Robert Swan, Registrar to the Bishop of Lincoln, who gave them to the Archaeological Institute at its Lincoln meeting in 1848. They were transferred to the British Museum in 1856.

31

DEATH AND BURIAL

The influx of Anglo–Saxons into Lincolnshire brought a new way of life ... and a new way of death. The Roman Christians had buried their dead (inhumation) without any possessions, for all were equal in the sight of their god. The Anglo–Saxons were pagans and brought their tradition of cremation, the ashes being buried in a pot along with gifts to establish their owner's status in the afterlife. The return of Christianity in the late 7th century re-introduced the practice of inhumation but the custom of leaving grave offerings persisted for a while and gives us a rare glimpse of the everyday objects of the time.

We know little of the settlements of this period and it is the cemeteries which give the most tangible evidence for the Anglo–Saxons in Lincolnshire; many such cemeteries are known, notably at Hough on the Hill, Ruskington and Sleaford. A few Anglo–Saxon burial mounds, assumed to be for important or wealthy individuals, have been discovered. The mound known as Cock Hill at Burgh le Marsh was excavated in 1933 and found to contain human bones and a 7th century buckle. More recent study has concluded that, whilst Cock Hill may have originated as a burial mound, it was later enlarged, perhaps as a mound for a windmill. It now has a broad hole in its top which is said to have been an arena for cock–fighting.

Cock Hill at Burgh le Marsh may have originated as a Saxon burial mound.

The Saxon minster of St. Mary's at Stow.

STOW MINSTER

North west Lincolnshire is particularly rich in Anglo-Saxon churches and St. Mary's at Stow must be one of the most memorable. It was founded by Bishop Aelfnoth in 975, possibly intended as the head minster (the mother church) for his diocese, which would explain its great size.

Alterations were made throughout the centuries and in Victorian times, the church, by then sadly decayed, was restored by the architect J. L. Pearson. An intriguing example of these alterations is the set of three windows in the south transept. One is Anglo-Saxon, one Norman, and one medieval. They are so close together that it seems as if each generation of masons was determined to out–do the last. St. Mary's contains some rare survivals from the early 13th Century. In the north transept parts of a painting showing St. Thomas Beckett have survived whilst, in the nave, a font decorated with 'pagan' symbols is guarded by a dragon coiled around its base.

ST. MARY LE WIGFORD, LINCOLN

In 597 Pope Gregory sent Augustine and a group of monks to 'preach the word of God to the English nation'. By 680, England had reverted to Christianity and the administrative units of the English church, the dioceses, were in place. The majority of early Anglo-Saxon churches were built of wood and have not survived, but Lincolnshire boasts a great wealth of later Anglo-Saxon church architecture. St. Mary Le Wigford in Lincoln is one of the best known of these – it has a typical late 11th century Anglo-Saxon tower with a tall round headed doorway and double belfry windows divided by a round pillar. The most unusual feature is an inscribed stone set into the tower to the right of the doorway. It is a Roman tombstone commemorating Sacer, son of Bruscus, probably found on the site when the church was built, for a Roman cemetery lies beneath the building. In the triangular space above the Roman inscription is a rare Anglo-Saxon dedication which, translated, reads *Eirtig had me built and endowed to the glory of Christ and St. Mary.*

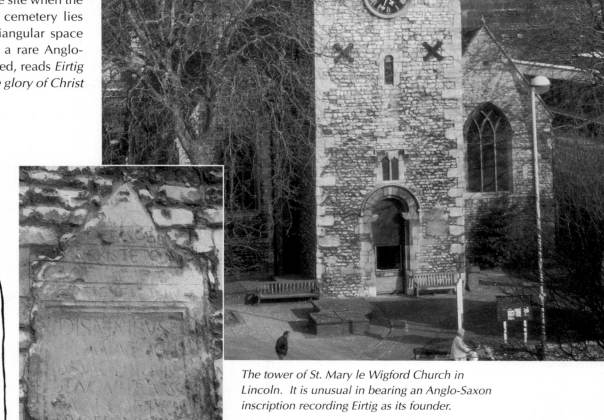

The tower of St. Mary le Wigford Church in Lincoln. It is unusual in bearing an Anglo-Saxon inscription recording Eirtig as its founder.

34

ANGLO–SAXON ARCHITECTURE

Lincolnshire is notable for its surviving Anglo-Saxon architecture, having almost 50 churches incorporating identifiable Anglo-Saxon features. Of particular note are Lincolnshire's late Anglo-Saxon church towers with their distinctive double belfry windows. Many of these may have been built after the Norman conquest, in the late 11th or early 12th centuries, but they still display the characteristic Anglo-Saxon style.

The earliest church which still survives is St. Peter's at Barton on Humber. It is thought that a 9th century timber church stood nearby, replaced in the 10th century by a stone church which consisted of a central tower (which was the nave) with a small chancel to the east and a baptistry to the west. The tower and baptistry still stand, their gable headed and round headed doors, windows and stripwork an impressive illustration

of classic Anglo-Saxon church architecture. The final stage was added to the tower in the 11th century when the Anglo-Saxon chancel was removed and replaced with a new nave and chancel, later remodelled in the 13th–15th centuries. St. Peter's became redundant in 1972; it is now owned by English Heritage and open to the public.

The tower of St. Margaret's church at Marton – a typical example of the many late Anglo–Saxon church towers in Lincolnshire. Note the double belfry windows and herringbone masonry.

The 10th century tower and baptistry of St. Peter's church at Barton on Humber.

ANGLO-SAXON REMAINS

Until the 1960s the Anglo-Saxons were almost invisible in the archaeological record. Indeed, this period had become know as The Dark Ages, owing to the lack of written histories and the scarcity of settlement remains. Archaeologists are now better able to recognise Anglo-Saxon settlement sites and an increasing number are being identified throughout the county. Nevertheless, the main class of objects in the museums comes from Anglo-Saxon cemetery sites. Until the re-introduction of Christianity the tradition of leaving grave goods with the dead flourished. These offerings were usually in the form of jewellery (brooches, buckles and beads) or equipment (pots, combs, knives, spears and shields). The objects, especially the jewellery, are often finely worked, showing outstanding craftsmanship, not at all indicative of a Dark Age.

LCC. Archaeology Collection.

Beads from an Anglo–Saxon cemetery at Welton discovered during construction of the Community Centre in 1971.

Sheffield Arts & Museums Department.

The hilt of the Fiskerton Sword, found in the River Witham in 1954.

Although weapons are relatively common in Anglo–Saxon graves, swords were highly prized as status symbols and are only found in richer graves. The Fiskerton Sword was found in the River Witham by a boy walking the river bank in 1954. It is a two–edged iron sword, its hilt decorated with silver bands mounted on a wood or bone handgrip which has disintegrated. The silver is engraved and was inlaid with 'niello' (a black paste of silver sulphide). The decoration includes geometric, plant and animal designs typical of the mid to late 9th century. The Fiskerton sword is now in Sheffield City Museum.

Although place–name evidence for the Viking presence in Lincolnshire is plentiful, archaeological evidence is slight. These metal objects found at Ketsby, near Alford, include a key, parts of stirrups and strap–ends which date from the Viking period and show characteristic designs.

Kevin Leahy, Scunthorpe Museum

Map showing the location of place-names ending in –by. Lincolnshire has the highest concentration in the country.

THE VIKINGS

The first Viking attacks on England occurred in the closing years of the 8th century, but it was not until the late 9th century that these Scandinavian raiders began to settle. In 886 a treaty with the English gave the Vikings the north and east of England, including the important towns of Lincoln and Stamford. It is clear that a great many Vikings settled in Lincolnshire for, although the archaeological evidence for them is slight, their presence in large numbers can be seen in the characteristic Viking place–names of the county. *By* was their word for any small settlement from a farm to a village (it has passed into English in by–law, a village law) and there are over 220 names ending –by in Lincolnshire; the greatest concentration in the country. Despite their violent beginnings, the Vikings seem to have integrated well into English society and, archaeologically, they are difficult to discern from their Anglo-Saxon neighbours. Occasionally, however, distinctive Scandinavian art styles incorporating stylised animals and leaves are found on everyday objects, testifying to the Viking presence.

INVADERS & SETTLERS
THE NORMANS
1066 – 1216

The south doorway of St. Andrew's Church at Sempringham, an exquisite example of Norman work. The doors, with wrought iron scroll–work, may also be of Norman date.

The Norman invasion of 1066, achieved with an army of fewer than 10,000 men, transformed the English political and administrative structure although it brought little in the way of new population. Following a decisive victory at the Battle of Hastings, William the Conqueror set about consolidating his new kingdom by displacing the Anglo–Saxon landowners and installing a Norman aristocracy. The new landlords were quick to stamp their authority on the countryside, constructing a network of castles and forts which remain to this day their most conspicuous addition to the English landscape. At least thirty such castles were built in Lincolnshire although few have survived to the present day. The Normans were generous in religious matters and encouraged the building of cathedrals and village churches, impressing their preference for Romanesque architecture on the local masons. Lincoln Cathedral was begun in the early 1070s and consecrated in 1092. Most of Lincolnshire's monasteries were founded at this time. A few were established in the early years of Norman rule, but it was during the first half of the 12th century that the majority came into being. By the close of the century there were over 80 religious houses in the county.

THE AGE OF THE MONASTERIES

The majority of the Anglo-Saxon monasteries in England were destroyed during the Viking raids of the 9th century and only a few (Crowland was one) struggled on in depleted state into the 11th century. The Normans, who were great patrons of the Church, founded a handful of new monasteries in England during the early years of the Conquest while the new aristocracy were preoccupied with securing their English estates and meeting their commitments to newly founded monasteries back home in Normandy. However, during the first quarter of the 12th century, there was a boom in monastery

foundation stimulated by the emergence of several new religious orders. In France, new austere orders, including the Cistercians, Carthusians, Augustinians and Premonstratensians, were formed, all of whom soon colonised Norman England. Here in Lincolnshire the only English order, the Gilbertines, was founded by St. Gilbert of Sempringham in 1131.

It became fashionable for the great landowning families to found monasteries as an expression of piety, and as a form of insurance policy to ensure the offering of prayers in perpetuity for their souls. By the close of the 12th century over

St. Leonard's Priory, Stamford, was founded around 1100 by monks from Durham. The surviving building represents about two thirds of the nave of the priory church. The west front and the arches of the north arcade are Norman work. The rest is a later repair and restoration.

80 abbeys and priories had been established in Lincolnshire and the county ranked as one of the most religious in the land.

ST. GILBERT OF SEMPRINGHAM

The church of St. Andrew's at Sempringham, once at the centre of a busy village in the shadow of a magnificent monastery, now stands alone in open fields.

St. Andrew's, built around 1100, was the first priory church of the only religious Order which originated wholly in England, the brainchild of a remarkable medieval Englishman, St. Gilbert of Sempringham. Born at Sempringham in 1083, the son of Jocelin, Norman knight and the lord of the manor, Gilbert studied abroad, returning home after several years to set up a school. On the death of his father in 1130, Gilbert became squire and priest of Sempringham and founded a convent for seven nuns at the church. Finding many other women and men wished to join, Gilbert formed a mixed community of monks and nuns – the first of its kind. A new priory was built on adjacent land and Gilbert asked the Cistercian Order to adopt the community. They suggested, instead, that he should form a new Order. So the Gilbertines came into being and prospered – by the Dissolution there were 26 Gilbertine Houses. Gilbert died at Sempringham in 1189 aged 106; he was made a saint in 1202. Sempringham Priory was dissolved in 1538 and the land passed to Lord Clinton who built a fine house there. Now the house and the village of Sempringham are gone with only a few faint bumps and hollows remaining to betray their presence.

The Church of St. Andrew's at Sempringham was the birthplace of St. Gilbert and the Gilbertines.

Boothby Pagnell Norman Manor House, near Grantham, was built around 1200 and is the best surviving example of its type in England.

BOOTHBY PAGNELL NORMAN MANOR HOUSE

By the close of the 12th century the houses built by the local lords were becoming more comfortable. Stone manor houses, defended by water filled moats, superseded their timber predecessors and the lord often provided a private room or 'solar' for himself and his family in addition to the main hall for his household. For added comfort and security these rooms were frequently built at first floor level above a vaulted basement, and entered by an external stairway. The best surviving example of this type in England is the manor house at Boothby Pagnell, 6.4 km (4 miles) from Grantham.

Boothby Pagnell manor house was built around 1200 (the west wing is much later) and is thought to be part of a larger complex which stood within a circular moat. The stone stairs lead up to the entrance into the main hall through which the solar is reached. The rectangular window is a later (15th century) replacement of the Norman original which was identical to the surviving twin arched window of the solar (on the right). The hall has a fireplace with a cylindrical chimney and a stone vaulted basement beneath the main rooms, with walls that are 1.2 metres thick.

The Norman House.

Ian George.

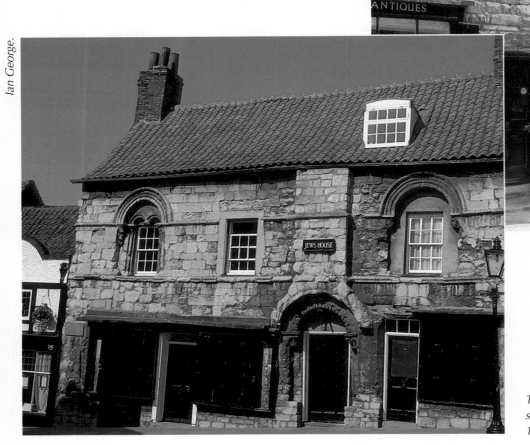

The Jews House in Lincoln – the earliest medieval stone residence in the city and the most famous 12th century house in England.

NORMAN HOUSES IN LINCOLN

The Jews House in Lincoln is considered to be one of the best surviving examples of Norman domestic architecture in the country. Stone houses were unusual in the 12th century and there is a tradition that they were built and owned by Jews who, by virtue of their wealth and unpopularity as moneylenders, required the extra security afforded by stone walls. Stone houses are also less susceptible to fire and perhaps this was a factor in the building of the Jews House (which was constructed around 1160) for a fire had destroyed much of Lincoln in 1122.

The Jews House is two storeyed with a steeply pitched roof. The lower floor once had arched openings for shops, later made rectangular. The entrance has a beautifully moulded Norman archway with a fireplace and flue incorporated into the wall above it. The original upper windows, although now modernised, still have their arches and traces of twin inner arches. A little further up Steep Hill there is another 12th century house (known as the Norman House) with a similar, but plainer, doorway. Its complete twin window, a restoration of 1878, gives a good impression of how the Jews House windows would originally have appeared.

LINCOLN CASTLE

Lincoln Castle was built on the orders of William the Conqueror when he passed through the town in 1068. For the site, he chose the south western corner of the upper Roman enclosure, and the Domesday Book records that 166 houses were demolished to make way for it. In the Norman style, a great mound of earth was thrown up and defended by a moat. There are two such mounds (or mottes) at Lincoln, which is most unusual, and it is now thought that the mound of Lucy Tower was the original Norman motte. The other motte, supporting the Observatory Tower, is believed to have been constructed in the mid 12th century. A defended enclosure (the inner bailey), formed by a great rampart of earth surrounded by a moat, was constructed on the lines of the present castle walls. The castle's outer bailey re-used the old Roman defences of the upper city, and this area is still known as the Bail today. Both the keep on the motte and the walls of the inner bailey were originally built of timber but were replaced in stone during the 12th century.

Although of Viking style, this stud is thought to be of Norman date. It was found during the excavation of the west gate of the Castle in 1992.

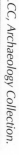

LCC, Archaeology Collection.

Lucy Tower, the Norman motte of Lincoln Castle.

The formidable ramparts at Castle Bytham.

Chris Cruickshank.

NORMAN CASTLES

The Normans perfected the use of military fortifications with the development of the 'instant castle' which could be built at great speed using local peasant labour and timber. These castles consisted of a mound of earth thrown up from a circular ditch with the top ringed by a wooden stockade defending a wooden tower. The mound, usually about 15 metres high, was called the motte and was encircled at ground level by another ditch and stockade enclosing an outer defensive area known as the bailey. The greatest threat to these early fortifications was fire, so, as time went by, timber structures were replaced by walls and towers of stone.

At first sight Lincolnshire does not appear to be a county of castles, yet there were at least 30 constructed here between the 11th and 13th centuries. Few were rebuilt in stone; perhaps more a reflection of the scarcity of suitable masonry than a comment on the tranquility of the county. Several impressive mottes remain, notably those at Lincoln, Castle Bytham and Barrow on Humber, whilst others (such as Stamford and Bourne) have virtually disappeared. Many Lincolnshire castles are modest in form, being no more than large, moated platforms, perhaps more properly termed ringworks, of which good examples may be seen at Swineshead, Heydour and Welbourn.

The Manwarings at Swineshead is a circular ringwork with two moats. A public footpath crosses the site.

THE KNIGHTS TEMPLAR

Among the many new religious orders which came into being in the 11th and 12th centuries was that of the Knights Templar, who originated at the time of the First Crusade after the capture of Jerusalem in 1099. The Templars were a military Order whose purpose was to guard the shrines of the Holy Land and protect pilgrims on the road. They acquired estates throughout Europe to fund their work, coming to Britain in 1128 to establish their main house at The Temple in London. In 1308 they were accused of heresy by King Philip IV of France and the Order was suppressed by the Pope in 1312.

Several Templar houses (known as preceptories) were founded in Lincolnshire, the best known example being that at Temple Bruer, near Sleaford. Templar churches often had a circular nave designed to imitate the church of the Holy Sepulchre in Jerusalem. Excavations at Temple Bruer in 1833 and 1907 discovered remains of just such a church with a short chancel flanked by two square towers. One of these towers still stands, repaired and re–roofed in 1912. On the ground floor there are stone seats *(sedilia)* around the walls and a spiral stair leading to the upper floors. The tower, now surrounded by a working farmyard, is open to the public.

The tower at Temple Bruer. The doorway would originally have opened into the chancel of the preceptory church.

NORMAN CHURCHES

The most familiar aspect of Norman architecture to survive in Lincolnshire is found in the numerous parish churches that were enlarged or rebuilt in the years following the Conquest. The naves of churches built or in use in the first half of the 11th century were usually smaller than those built after the Conquest, and by the 12th century many churches were altered to increase the size of the nave. There does not seem to have been any significant population increase to necessitate these enlargements – they are probably a reflection of the wealth and prestige of the local lord. Most commonly an aisle was added, usually on the north side of the nave. This was done by building onto the existing north side and piercing the old wall with a series of arches supported on columns. Norman arcades with round headed arches, sturdy columns and simple decoration survive in many churches. Other characteristic features of Norman church architecture still to be seen, are south doorways, their round arches carved with zigzags, beaks or twisted rope mouldings.

The Norman arcade in Coleby Church.

The drum shaped font at Coleby, decorated with interlocking arches, is typically Norman.

MEDIEVAL LEGACY

Medieval Lincolnshire did not exist as such; the county as we know it was then divided into three areas – Holland, Kesteven and Lindsey, each with distinct administrative, geographical and agricultural characters. The early part of the period was generally prosperous, and great quantities of wool (much of which was produced by the abbeys and priories) and salt (produced at coastal salterns) were exported to the continent through Lindsey and Holland ports. Principal among these was Boston; the town 'built on wool' which was exporting the fleeces of around 3 million sheep annually at the end of the 13th century. Boston's 'Stump', as the Church tower of St. Botolph is affectionately known, was built during the 14th century largely from the proceeds of this trade, as were many of the fine stone churches in the Wolds and Fens. The special status, sturdy construction and communal care of these buildings has helped ensure their survival to the present day but other, more ordinary structures have fared less well. Often the only traces of the homes of small farmers and peasants are the grassy humps and hollows of deserted villages, abandoned after decades of failing harvests, economic change and the Black Death.

The massive parish church of St. Botolph at Boston, built in the early 14th century, has become a symbol of South Lincolnshire. Its tower (known to all as the 'Stump') is visible for miles around and once helped guide ships to this prosperous medieval port.

LINCOLN CATHEDRAL

The 'jewel in the crown' of the county's heritage, Lincoln Cathedral watches over the city through a pair of remarkable medieval windows; the 'Dean's Eye' in the north transept, and the 'Bishop's Eye' in the south. Work on the Cathedral began in 1072, under the direction of Bishop Remigius. It continued, despite a severe fire and an earthquake, until well into the medieval period. The passage of time is marked by changes in style – from the great semi–circular Norman doorway on the west front to the lofty vaulting and flowing tracery of the medieval Angel Choir. This was built to house the shrine of St. Hugh, the Bishop of Lincoln who was canonised in 1220. The ornate oak stalls in St. Hugh's choir date from the 14th century, and under each seat, or misericord, is a different carved figure. Perhaps the most famous carving, however, is that of the Lincoln Imp perched high in the Angel Choir, a traditional symbol of good luck.

Lincoln Cathedral at night, from the north. The Dean's Eye, the great circular window of the north transept, is under repair.

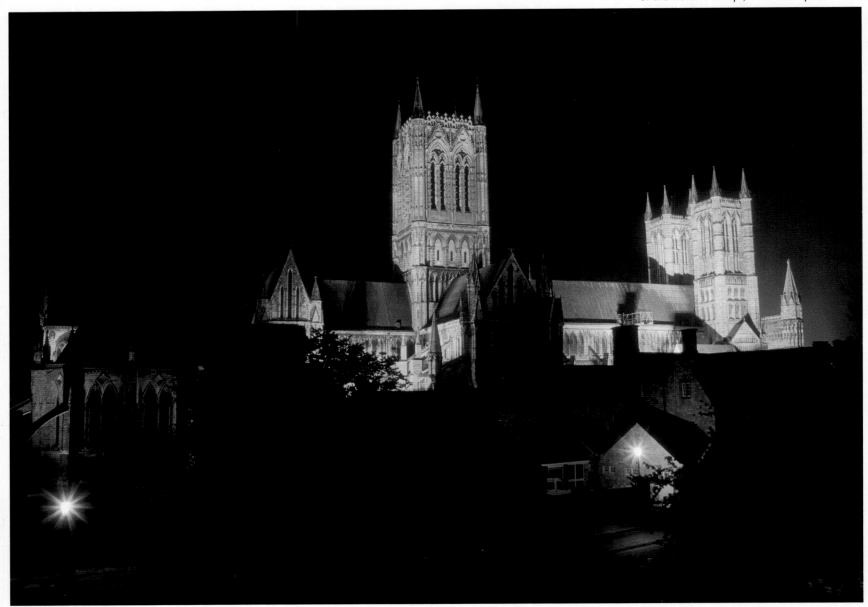

THE CATHEDRAL CLOSE

Lincoln's Anglo-Saxon minster was contained within the walls of the old Roman town but when Remigius built the Norman cathedral on the site in 1072 part of the old town wall had to be removed. In 1255 the east end of the cathedral was extended to include St. Hugh's shrine and the town's defences were again disturbed. The paths and lanes around the cathedral precinct became a notorious haunt of robbers and murderers and, in 1285, Bishop Oliver Sutton obtained permission from King Edward I to build a wall, 3.6 metres high, to protect the precinct, thus creating the Cathedral Close. Some stretches of the wall still survive, notably along East Bight, and two wall towers can still be seen in Winnowsty Lane. Of the five main gates to the Close, which were guarded and locked at nights, two still stand at Exchequergate and Pottergate. Pottergate, which is now isolated in a traffic island, was 'restored' in 1884. The chamber over the single narrow carriageway once housed a portcullis and was equipped with a fireplace and garderobe (toilet).

Pottergate arch, the southern entrance to the Cathedral Close, is a Victorian restoration of the 14th century gatehouse.

THE STONEBOW

There has been a gateway on this site since Roman times for this was the main entrance to *Lindum Colonia*, where Ermine Street entered the lower Roman city. The Roman gateway probably formed the basis of the medieval gate, demolished in the late 14th century when it became unsafe. In 1390 Richard II ordered a new arch to be built but the work was not completed until 1520. The Stonebow, as originally constructed, consisted of a central carriageway with smaller archways each side for pedestrians. At the front (south side), the main thoroughfare is flanked by two figures set in recesses: they are, on the left, the Virgin Mary, Patron Saint of the City, and on the right, the Archangel Gabriel. Over the main arch are the arms of James I commemorating his visit to Lincoln in 1617. Restoration and alteration in Victorian times (to mark the 1887 Golden Jubilee) opened up an additional pedestrian archway on the west side.

Since the 16th century the ground and first floors of the Stonebow have been let to local traders. The whole of the second floor is occupied by the Guildhall, a magnificent room used from the outset as the Council Chamber of the City of Lincoln.

The Stonebow, on the site of the Roman gateway to the city, was built in the 15th century. It houses the Guildhall, used as the Council Chamber of the City of Lincoln, and the City's Civic Insignia.

The secluded church of St. Leonard, Kirkstead.

'EARLY ENGLISH' AND 'DECORATED' STYLES

Building styles changed throughout the medieval period, and Kirkstead and Heckington churches demonstrate the first two phases of that change. Tucked away behind the stark ruin of Kirkstead Abbey is the tiny church of St. Leonard. It was probably built around 1230 as a chantry chapel, where prayers would be said for the soul of its founder, Robert of Tattershall. The style is 'Early English', and very simple, with narrow pointed openings and carving around the door and windows only.

The Church of St. Andrew, at Heckington, was built about a century later in a new and ornate style, aptly called 'decorated'. The parapets are rich with gargoyles and the windows are large with inventive flowing tracery. St. Andrew's greatest glory is, however, its stone carving. Christ in Majesty watches over the south porch whilst inside the Easter Sepulchre, with its remarkable carvings of Christ, the Marys and the sleeping soldiers, is a year–round reminder of the Easter story.

The Church of St. Andrew in Heckington.

THE 'PERPENDICULAR' STYLE

The two churches of St. James', Louth and Holy Trinity, Tattershall, were built within a few decades of each other in the mid 15th century. They are both 'perpendicular' in style, that is with the emphasis on vertical lines, particularly in the windows. The churches were both founded on wealth – in Louth, the wealth of the Guilds and local people and in Tattershall, that of Ralph, Lord Cromwell, Treasurer of England. There the similarities end, for whilst Louth church is richly ornamented with flying buttresses and decorated pinnacles, Tattershall seems austere by comparison. The character of Holy Trinity is perhaps best appreciated inside, for as sunshine floods through the large windows, the walls seem almost to be made of glass, leaving only slender stone piers to support the great weight of the roof. The most abiding feature of St. James', however, must surely be its graceful steeple, decorated with crockets (leafy knobs) which are spaced further apart as they go up, creating an illusion of regularity from the ground.

St. James' Church, Louth.

The Collegiate Church of the Holy Trinity, Tattershall.

MONASTIC RUINS

The monasteries played a leading role in the economic life of medieval Lincolnshire becoming, collectively, one of the major landowners, employers, and traders in the county. Their extensive estates (the products of gifts from pious donors) were managed through a network of granges (monastic farms) which produced wool for export throughout Europe. The monasteries prospered greatly from this trade until the introduction of the wool tax in the late 13th century. By this time there were over 120 priories, friaries, abbeys, preceptories and hospitals in Lincolnshire, representing most of the religious Orders of the time.

Given the scale of monastic buildings, and their former numbers, it is at first puzzling as to why so little remains. Today Lincolnshire is virtually devoid of abbey ruins. By comparison, the monastic ruins of Yorkshire are truly monumental – but there, building stone is plentiful and the ruins more remote.

The gatehouse of Thornton Abbey, built around 1380, is one of the finest and earliest large scale brick buildings in the country. It probably owes its survival to its brick construction for the abbey itself was dismantled, much of its stone going to build Ferriby Sluice.

David Stocker.

One wall of the refectory was left standing at Tupholme Abbey, including this pulpit set into the wall. These were later modified, probably in the early 18th century, to serve as picturesque features for the newly built Tupholme Hall.

A great crag of masonry, a fragment of the south transept wall, is all that remains of the Cistercian abbey church at Kirkstead. Perhaps it was just too dangerous to demolish?

Monastic buildings were not necessarily demolished at the Dissolution. Generally, the lead was removed from the roofs, and some churches were demolished, but many of the other buildings must have remained standing. Often they were converted into country mansions by succeeding owners but few of these houses weathered the changing fashions of the 18th and 19th centuries and most were abandoned. The stone, a valuable commodity in Lincolnshire, was carted off to build new houses, farms and barns. Limestone not used for re–building was burnt to make lime for fertiliser and for building. Most abbey sites in Lincolnshire now have only grassy mounds to mark where the buildings once stood. Those ruins that do survive were either too difficult or dangerous to dismantle or, perhaps, survived just long enough to become valued as picturesque features in the landscape.

STANDING STONE CROSSES

In many villages of Lincolnshire, among the gravestones or in a forgotten corner beside the village green, stand the remains of a stone cross. Often only the base and a stump of the shaft survive, although some have been restored in recent times as village features or war memorials. Most of these standing crosses were erected during the medieval period and served a variety of functions. In churchyards they were stopping places for outdoor religious processions, particularly those connected with Palm Sunday; at other times they were sites for preaching,

public proclamation and penance. Crosses were also erected in market places where their presence sanctioned business dealings and later provided a focal point for municipal ceremonies and official announcements.

The commonest type of standing cross has a stepped base with the cross–shaft set in a socket stone (some of which are carved or inscribed) on the uppermost step. The cross–shafts are usually square or octagonal. The cross–heads took many forms from simple crucifixes to

elaborate lantern shaped structures. Very few original cross–heads survive as they were considered to be papist symbols at the time of the Reformation and were systematically destroyed during the 16th and 17th centuries.

The base of Silk Willoughby cross has carvings symbolising the four gospels around its base. The carvings, which are now very worn, are of a man for St. Matthew, a winged lion for St. Mark, a winged calf for St. Luke and an eagle for St. John (shown).

The medieval village cross at North Kyme stands about three metres high.

DESERTED MEDIEVAL VILLAGES

At the time of the Domesday Survey (1086) Lincolnshire was one of the most densely populated counties. Between the 11th and 14th centuries the population more than doubled and by the early 14th century the towns and villages were becoming overcrowded. A series of events then combined to bring about a steady decline in the county's fortunes. Changes in climate and farming methods, and the onset of the Black Death in 1349, led to widespread depopulation of the countryside and the end of many Lincolnshire villages.

There are at least 235 deserted medieval villages scattered across Lincolnshire, the majority on the Wolds and the South Kesteven uplands. Many of these village sites appear now as bumps and hollows in the fields and it is often possible to trace the outlines of the streets, houses and gardens. Sometimes the ruins of the church still stand, as at Calceby, near Alford. Calceby, which survived the Black Death, could not survive the change of land–use from arable to sheep farming which took place during the 15th and 16th centuries. Some dwellings remained until the early years of this century but now only the gaunt ruin of St. Andrew's church bears witness to the once busy streets.

The white skeleton of Calceby Church sits on a knoll close by the ancient Bluestone Heath Road. In the fields around it lie the bumps and hollows that tell of a once thriving village, now long abandoned.

Chris Cruickshank.

Ridge and furrow field systems at South Reston near Louth. A medieval manor house once stood on the rectangular moated area to the right of the farmyard.

RIDGE AND FURROW

By the 11th century one third of England was ploughland, most of it comprising large open fields surrounding the medieval villages. The fields were subdivided into strips which were owned or rented by peasant farmers; the ownership and use of strips being controlled by manorial courts or village assemblies. Strip farming began in late Anglo-Saxon times and survived until the 18th century. The visible remains of strip farming can still be seen throughout Lincolnshire in the form of 'ridge (or rig) and furrow', parallel, sinuous undulations surviving in old pasture. The ridges were formed by many years of ploughing up one side of the ridge and down the other resulting in a linear bank. The effect may originally have been accidental but it had advantages both for drainage and for the delineation of land–holdings and so was probably continued intentionally. The ridges do not in themselves indicate the 'strips' which could consist of several ridges and furrows. Although much of Lincolnshire's landscape was once covered in ridge and furrow, modern intensive agriculture has levelled the majority and it is becoming increasingly rare.

MY HOME IS MY CASTLE

In the late medieval period readily defensible homes for the rich and powerful were no longer a strict necessity, but the castle style, with some concessions to domestic convenience, was still popular, proclaiming the wealth and status of the occupier.

Tattershall Castle, built of brick (then an expensive and prestigious material), was erected in the mid 15th century for Ralph, Lord Cromwell, High Treasurer of England. The impressive keep, which was extensively restored in 1912–14, has four principal floors, each with a central hall, connected by a spiral staircase in the south east turret. The roof has two levels, giving access to the machicolations – holes through which missiles could be dropped onto an enemy below. However, the large pointed windows which light the main halls show that the Castle's main function was not defensive, for they would offer little resistance to a speeding cannon ball!

Tattershall Castle is owned by the National Trust and is open to the public.

The Tower on the Moor stands on Woodhall golf course, north east of the town centre.

Rochford Tower, on the outskirts of Boston, is privately owned.

The defensive tower–house, usually associated with the north–country, was also popular in Lincolnshire. In addition to Tattershall Castle, there are examples in Woodhall Spa and Boston. The Tower on the Moor, just outside Woodhall Spa, was built by Lord Cromwell some years after the Castle, perhaps to serve as a hunting lodge. The surviving stair turret, about 18 metres high, is a good example of late medieval brickwork.

In Boston, Hussey and Rochford Towers were both built in the 15th century, and were originally part of larger houses. The Hussey family were once prominent in the area, but Lord Hussey's execution in 1536 following his failure to deal with the Lincolnshire Rising marked the beginning of a rapid decline in their fortunes. Members of the Rochford family served their county several times as Knights of the Shire and High Sheriffs, holding their estate until the end of the 16th century.

David Stocker.

Gainsborough Old Hall, dating from the last half of the 15th century.

LATE MEDIEVAL HOUSES

From the late medieval period we begin to see the survival of large, non-defensive houses in the county. At Gainsborough Old Hall the fortified tradition, although here used for display, still echoes in the great octagonal tower. Medieval brickwork is also visible on the striking range of chimneys, with adjoining garderobe (toilet) chutes and crow–stepped gables. This house, with its remarkable timber–framed open hall, was built for the Burgh family, who enjoyed spectacular rises and falls in prosperity under royal patronage.

Ayscoughfee Hall, at the other end of the county in Spalding, is thought to have been built for Sir Richard Aldwyn in 1429. Again, some fine medieval brickwork has survived, especially in the recently revealed vaulted staircase. The Hall has been much altered through time; in the 18th century by the Reverend Maurice Johnson, grandson of the founder of the Spalding Gentlemen's Society. Fittingly, it now houses the Museum of South Holland, managed by the District Council.

Ayscoughfee Hall. Many of the 'gothic' features on the west front date from the 1845 alterations.

PIETY AND MAGNIFICENCE

On the southern fringe of the county, Browne's Hospital in Stamford and Crowland Abbey reflect both piety and the desire to create earthly magnificence out of stone.

Crowland Abbey is the fourth such building on the site, and was founded in honour of St. Guthlac, an 8th century monk. The abbey suffered fires, an earthquake, and much demolition following its dissolution in 1539. The 15th century north aisle, surrounded by evocative ruins, has survived and is now the Parish Church.

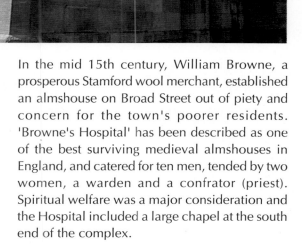

Browne's Hospital, Broad Street, Stamford.

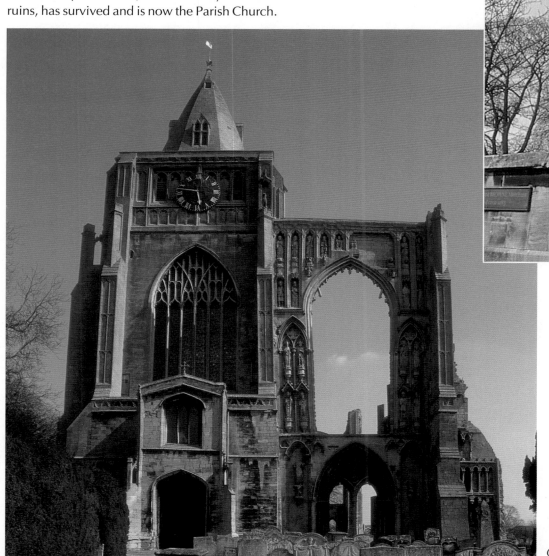

In the mid 15th century, William Browne, a prosperous Stamford wool merchant, established an almshouse on Broad Street out of piety and concern for the town's poorer residents. 'Browne's Hospital' has been described as one of the best surviving medieval almshouses in England, and catered for ten men, tended by two women, a warden and a confrator (priest). Spiritual welfare was a major consideration and the Hospital included a large chapel at the south end of the complex.

Crowland Abbey, on the southern border of the county.

61

Julian's Bower on the Cliff edge at Alkborough is the only surviving turf maze in Lincolnshire.

THE ALKBOROUGH MAZE

Turf mazes or labyrinths are rare and curious structures. They are usually circular, formed by a raised turf pathway in complex spiral shape leading from a single entrance, through many twists and turns, to the centre. For many centuries they have been used for games and amusement, although their original purpose may have been more formal. These mazes are often called *Julian's Bower* or *Troy Town* for it is said that Julius, son of Aeneas (the founder of Rome) brought the idea from Troy to Italy.

Four mazes are recorded in Lincolnshire at Appleby, Louth, Horncastle and Alkborough, but only the Alkborough maze survives today. It is 13.4 metres in diameter, its intricate pattern cut 150mm into the turf of the Cliff edge. The location gives a breathtaking view across the Trent Falls where the Ouse and Trent join to form the Humber.

No–one knows for certain what the maze was for or when it was made. It is first recorded in the late 17th century but its origins may lie in the 12th century when Benedictine monks from Spalding established a grange nearby. One suggestion is that it was used for the performance of religious penance, sinners being required to walk its tortuous path with dried peas in their boots.

─TUDORS & STEWARTS─

Torksey Castle.

The era which began with King Henry VII's accession, and ended with Queen Anne's death in 1714, saw far–reaching changes in the social, religious and political life of the county. Lincolnshire took its place on the national stage more than once in these turbulent times. In 1536, county men and women were so enraged by King Henry VIII's plans to dissolve the minor monasteries and raise taxes that they rebelled. The 'Lincolnshire Rising', as the event came to be known, was a brief but strongly felt challenge to royal authority. In the Civil War, however, the Royal forces were defeated at the Battle of Winceby (1643) by Cromwell's Parliamentarian army. There were peaceful times too, and developments in agriculture and transport began the slow process of change in the countryside which was to culminate in the Georgian period. The gradual embrace of Renaissance ideas and philosophies began to change the way people viewed themselves in relation to God and the universe. One of Lincolnshire's chief proponents in this new spirit of investigation was Sir Isaac Newton, born at Woolsthorpe Manor in 1642.

ELIZABETHAN HOUSES

The grand Elizabethan houses of Doddington Hall and Torksey Castle show similarities in style and material, but have survived in dramatically different states of repair. Torksey Castle was built for Sir Robert Jermyn around 1560, on the east bank of the River Trent. It held a strategically important site near a crossing point on the river, but in the Civil War this position proved the downfall of the Castle. In July 1645, the potential stronghold was burnt down by the Newark Royalists and has remained a ruin ever since.

Doddington Hall, however, has been the subject of a major restoration programme since the 1950s, and proudly displays its treasures to the public. It was built around 1600 for Thomas Tailor of Lincoln by the renowned Elizabethan architect Robert Smythson. The plan resembles a double E, and each storey is focused on a great room. On the third floor that room is the Long Gallery which, at 29 metres long, was used for wet–weather recreation and even for indoor bowls.

Torksey Castle, on the bank of the River Trent.

Doddington Hall, near Lincoln.

JACOBEAN HOUSES

During the Jacobean period (early 17th century) a number of smaller but still substantial houses were built for prosperous gentry such as the Fishers of Bourne and well–to–do farmers like the Newtons of Woolsthorpe. Woolsthorpe Manor, built around 1623 of Ancaster stone with a Collyweston slate roof, displays the typical mullioned windows of the period. It is famous as the birthplace of Sir Isaac Newton who, while staying there to escape the plague of 1665 in Cambridge, carried out his ground–breaking work on the laws of gravity, differential calculus, and the refraction of light.

Woolsthorpe Manor, near Colsterworth, birthplace of Sir Isaac Newton – now a National Trust property and open to the public.

The Red Hall, restored in the 1960s by Bourne United Charities.

The Red Hall is a large red–brick and stone–dressed mansion, probably built for Gilbert Fisher around 1610. The main accommodation was contained within the house, but outside there was also a brew–house, dairy–house, and, following an old tradition, an 'out–kitchen'. The history of the Hall took an unusual twist when, in 1860, it was sold to the Bourne and Essendine Railway Company and became a booking office and station master's house.

COUNTRY HOUSES

Belton House was built in 1685 for 'Young' Sir John Brownlow, who had just inherited a fortune from his great–uncle, 'Old' Sir John. The house was built from mellow Ancaster stone quarried at nearby Heydour, and nearly two million bricks, made on Belton Heath. Designed with restrained elegance, the house has some well–placed decorative touches, like the cupola (small dome) and roof balustrade. These were removed in a spirit of severe classicism during 18th century alterations, but were replaced in the 19th century.

In its setting of gardens, parkland, church and estate village, Belton House seems the essence of tranquility. This has not, however, always been the case, for in the 1930s both the Prince of Wales and Wallis Simpson stayed there, and Lord Brownlow played an important part in the Abdication crisis. In the 1990s Belton was again on the national stage, this time as a setting for the BBC adaptation of Jane Austen's novel, 'Pride and Prejudice'.

Belton House, near Grantham, is a National Trust property and open to the public.

EARLY JOURNEYS

Transport has changed greatly since Tudor and Stewart times. Then, travellers went on foot or horse–back, and goods were often carried by packhorse. Some of the old packhorse bridges, with their shallow gradients and cobbled surfaces still survive.

The distances travelled in a day were short, and overnight stops were made at inns. The Angel and Royal in Grantham is one of the oldest, and has an ornate 15th century facade. Originally known as 'The Angel', it was probably owned by the Knights Hospitaller in the 14th century, and has since sheltered some important visitors. Whilst staying here in 1483 Richard III signed the death warrant of the Duke of Buckingham, and in 1633 King Charles I was a guest. The 'Royal' was added to the name in 1866 for a visit by the Prince of Wales (later Edward VII). The inn's position on the Great North Road bought it more general prosperity in the 18th century, when hundreds of coaches visited it each week.

The Angel and Royal in Grantham. A tradition of hospitality which stretches back for centuries.

Packhorse bridges at West Rasen (left) and Utterby.

Mud and stud cottage in Thimbleby.

MUD AND STUD

Our perception of a period is inclined to be coloured by what has survived, and from the 17th and 18th centuries this has tended to be the larger, more substantial houses, probably because they were built of expensive, more durable materials.

Most of the population, however, lived in more cramped conditions, in humble dwellings like this 'mud and stud' cottage in Thimbleby. A 'mud and stud' building is literally made of just that; 'studs', or rough timber gathered locally and jointed to make a frame, which is then filled in with 'mud', a mixture of earth, lime, straw and animal hair. This method was traditional to Lincolnshire, and was inexpensive and relatively straightforward. The roofs were usually thatched, and the window openings very small, as glass was a rarely afforded luxury.

The tide of progress has swept many of these buildings away, but a renewed interest in vernacular architecture has led to protection for some of the survivors.

LORD CROMWELL'S BUILDINGS

When Ralph, Lord Cromwell began his extensive building programme in Tattershall in the mid 15th century, he did not neglect the well–being of the poor. Included in Henry VI's licence of 1439 was permission to rebuild the almshouses, which were to house thirteen poor old people of either sex. Like those in Stamford, the Tattershall almshouses included a chapel to ensure the piety of the inhabitants, who also had to wear a livery of frise–russet (rough, reddish–brown) cloth. The almshouses (now called the Bede Cottages) were remodelled on the same site in the 17th and 19th centuries. At some stage the original ten units have been combined to form five bigger dwellings.

Not far from the Bede Cottages stands the Old College, part of the Grammar School that was commissioned by Lord Cromwell and completed after his death by Bishop Waynflete. The school served the church choristers and the sons of Lord Cromwell's tenants, and is reputed to have included the composer John Taverner among its pupils. In 1790 it was converted to a malting house and granary, and continued to have an economic use until the middle of this century.

The Bede Cottages (Almshouses), close by the church at Tattershall, were founded by Lord Cromwell in the 15th century but later remodelled.

The ruins of the 15th century Old College at Tattershall are in the guardianship of English Heritage and managed by Heritage Lincolnshire. The site is open to the public.

TUDOR EDUCATION

During this period the great majority of the population could neither read nor write. Education was the province of those with the means to pay for a personal tutor or a place at a private school.

There was, however, a growing interest in learning, and in 1484 the Bishop of Winchester founded the Magdalen College in his home town, Wainfleet All Saints. The new brick school, which cost the princely sum of £27 to build, was austere in style. Its design was probably influenced by similar buildings around the county as the architect was Henry Albroke of Tattershall.

The scholars were all boys, Latin was the chief language, and reading, writing, arithmetic and 'good manners' were the main subjects. It was, no doubt, the Bishop's intention that the Magdalen School should provide a steady supply of pupils for his other foundation, the Magdalen College at Oxford University.

Magdalen College, Wainfleet, now used as a museum and public library.

WREN LIBRARY, LINCOLN CATHEDRAL

After the great fire of London had destroyed the old St. Paul's in 1666, the new Cathedral, and many other city churches, were built to the designs of Sir Christopher Wren, then the country's most eminent architect.

Lincolnshire people can see a fine example of Wren's work closer to home as, in 1660, he was commissioned to design a new library for Lincoln Cathedral. The order came from the Dean, Michael Honeywood, who was an enthusiastic collector of books. The result was an elegant first floor room supported on an arcade of classical arches, which replaced the ruined north side of the cloister. Wren also specified the design for the inside of the library which was recently restored to its original colour scheme of muted green and blue with touches of gold, by students from the Lincoln College of Art and Design.

The Wren Library at Lincoln Cathedral can be visited by appointment.

THE CIVIL WAR IN LINCOLNSHIRE

Lincolnshire came into national prominence in 1643, when a major battle of the Civil War was fought at Winceby, near Horncastle.

The Royalist garrison was stationed at Bolingbroke Castle, a moated stronghold built around 1220 for Ranulph de Blundevill, Earl of Chester. In the 14th century, the Castle was the birthplace of Henry Bolingbroke, later Henry IV. In October 1643, however, it was under siege by the Parliamentarians. Royalist forces coming to aid their beleaguered allies were met at Winceby, two miles from the castle, by the opposition under the command of Thomas Fairfax, Lord Manchester, and Lieut. Gen. Cromwell. The two sides drew up and charged; the battle was swift but bloody. The Royalists were routed, some say with 200 killed and 200 taken prisoner. Bolingbroke Castle was subsequently destroyed by the Parliamentarians, to prevent it being used against them in the future. Today, the valley where 'blood ran down horse fetlock deep' is peaceful countryside, but the memory lives on in the name, 'Slash Hollow'.

Bolingbroke Castle is in the guardianship of English Heritage and managed by the Heritage Trust of Lincolnshire.

An 'erratic', a giant stone moved during the glacial period, at Slash Hollow on the site of the Battle of Winceby.

GEORGIAN ELEGANCE

Gunby Hall, dating from around 1700, is a National Trust property.

The Georgian period was one of great change and development, in Lincolnshire as well as in the rest of the country. As the Industrial Revolution gathered pace, the county's common lands were enclosed, and Fens drained, beginning the process that was to turn Lincolnshire into the 'larder' of the country. Improvements in transport, through the establishment of turnpike trusts and navigable waterways made travel and trade more efficient, whilst the communication of ideas was made easier through increased literacy and the development of newspapers and 'improvement' societies. The French Revolution(s) of 1789 (and

1830) sent shock waves through the English aristocracy, but although English labourers suffered great hardships in years of poor harvests, falling corn prices and cholera epidemics, some measure of reform was achieved peaceably here, through the electoral Reform Bill of 1832 and the gradual acceptance of non–conformist religion.

The legacy of this period can be seen in the elegant Georgian townhouses and graceful country houses found around the county, though their air of calm and serenity sometimes belies the fast–moving period that created them.

The Temple at Coleby Hall is privately owned and is not normally open to the public.

Fydell House was acquired and restored by the Boston Preservation Trust in 1935.

THE CLASSICAL STYLE

The 18th century style is recognised for its emphasis on regularity, proportion and classical echoes. Fydell House, Boston, with its sash windows and Doric pilasters around the door is an early example of the type. The house was built for Samuel Jackson, and in 1726 it was bought by Joseph Fydell, who promptly placed his initials on its frontage. The Fydells were a prominent Boston family who later found fame as vintners, and whose members served several times as Mayors of the town.

The Temple of Romulus and Remus in the grounds of Coleby Hall is a notable example of Georgian architecture, this time in the Neo–Classical style. It was designed in 1762 for Thomas Scrope by the famous architect Sir William Chambers, and has a coffered ceiling (a honeycomb of sunken panels) inside the dome. The fashion for classical buildings dedicated to ancient gods, artfully sited in landscaped parks, was central to the 'picturesque' style of gardening, inspired by paintings by Poussin and Claude Lorrain among others.

GEORGIAN COUNTRY HOUSES

Lincolnshire can boast many fine examples of elegant Georgian country houses, artfully sited in parkland to make the most of the natural and man–made landscape.

Fulbeck Hall is one such, set in the undulations of the Lincoln Edge. It has been the home of the Fane family for nearly 400 years, although most of the present house was built in 1733 following a disastrous fire which left only the service wing standing. The Hall had a significant role in the second world war, for it was requisitioned by the army and used as the headquarters for the 1st Airborne Division.

Fillingham Castle, occupies an impressive Cliff-top position. It is a private house but can be viewed from a public footpath.

Fulbeck Hall is open to the public on selected dates, and contains a museum to the 1st Airborne Division and their part in the Battle of Arnhem.

A grand entrance gate on Ermine Street (A15) north of Lincoln signals the presence of Fillingham Castle, but the house, on the edge of the Lincoln Cliff, is perhaps better appreciated from the lower B1398. It was built around 1770 for Sir Cecil Wray, in the 'Gothick' castellated style then popular. The architect is thought to have been John Carr of York, who also designed nearby Norton Place.

Gate Burton 'Chateau', clearly visible from the A156 to Gainsborough, is a grandiose summer house built in 1747 in the grounds of Gate Burton Hall.

GATE BURTON'S CHATEAU

Many travellers on the A156 south of Gainsborough will have wondered at the sight of a small, toy–like building perched on a grassy mound overlooking the River Trent. Known variously as the Gazebo, the Temple, or the 'Shatoo' (Chateau), this is actually a folly built as a landscape feature in 1747. It was designed by the architect John Platt for the Gainsborough lawyer Thomas Hutton, who had just bought Gate Burton estate from the Earl of Abingdon. The red–brick hall, with its finely tooled stone ornamentation, was not built until 1768, and Thomas Hutton apparently used the Chateau as his weekend country retreat until the main house was finished. The Chateau was then used as a summer house, a shooting lodge, and accommodation for estate workers with, reputedly, an outside staircase leading to the bedroom. It has recently been repaired by the Landmark Trust and is available as holiday accommodation.

GEORGIAN TOWNHOUSES IN SPALDING

In the early years of the 19th century new housing developments were built in Spalding, some extending along the River Welland to the south of the busy port area, which centred around Double Street. Welland Terrace, on London Road, was probably erected by local builder John Cunnington, and followed the latest style of three storeys with a regular arrangement of sash windows and elegant door–cases.

The harmony and grand proportions of the Terrace would no doubt have appealed to members of the town's prosperous middle class, for it allowed them to boast of an impressive address, whilst only requiring them to pay for a small part of it!

Despite their modernity, when built the terraced houses would have been lit by lamps and candles, for the town gasworks were not built until 1832. Sanitation too, may have been a problem, for Spalding did not get its own waterworks until 1860. Until then, householders had to buy water from carriers (at $\frac{1}{2}$d for $3\frac{1}{2}$ gallons in 1850), or risk pollution and disease by using the river or a well.

Spalding's Welland Terrace, an elegant row of Georgian townhouses now happily supplied with 20th century conveniences.

Bourne Town Hall.

GEORGIAN PUBLIC BUILDINGS

Increased prosperity in the early 19th century encouraged the construction of public buildings. In 1821 nearly £1400 was raised from subscriptions and rate increases to build a Town Hall in Bourne. The new building was designed by Bryan Browning, and housed the Quarter and Petty Sessions, incorporating a set of trade stalls (or 'shambles') underneath. Its ingenious design includes a grand outside staircase, which sweeps behind a pair of classical columns, an idea borrowed from Roman baths.

Boston Assembly Rooms, still used for social gatherings.

Boston Assembly Rooms, built in 1822, is another grand public building, this time with a social function, housing banquets, balls and card assemblies. It was commissioned by the powerful Boston Corporation, established in 1545 to replace the medieval guilds. The Corporation was a self–electing body and its views did not always agree with those of other citizens. In 1831, dragoons had to be called in to subdue protesters, led by drum and fife, who were demonstrating against the Corporation in the Market Place. The electoral reforms which they were seeking were achieved fairly peaceably in 1832.

CRIME AND PUNISHMENT

Not all Georgian public buildings had as pleasant a function as the Assembly Rooms. In 1825, the architect Bryan Browning, already responsible for Bourne Town Hall, designed the Folkingham House of Correction, also known as the Gaol. The surviving part is the former gate and governor's house, and the earthen banks to either side are part of the old castle bailey, which occupied the site until the mid 16th century.

The 1825 building replaced an earlier House of Correction on the village green which had been

in use since 1609. Internment could be for a variety of reasons, some born of desperation. In 1740, for example, there was a riot in Bourne against the export of corn from the town in a time of great shortage. The disturbance was quelled and five women were imprisoned at Folkingham.

The new premises could accommodate up to 70 prisoners in solitary cells, and included a treadmill which was used until the gaol closed in 1877.

Folkingham House of Correction was repaired and converted for holiday use in 1987 by the Landmark Trust.

THE LAWN, LINCOLN

Until the first half of the 19th century, treatment of the mentally ill had generally been rudimentary, and often brutal. In 1819, however, a new asylum was built on a three acre site just outside the Castle walls in Lincoln. It was here, that a new, more humane method of treatment was pioneered by Dr. E. Charlesworth. He prohibited the use of such instruments as the 'Whirling Chair' and the 'Bath of Surprise' but was best known for his crusade against the use of solitary confinement and restraint (the strait jacket) in the treatment of disturbed patients.

'The Lawn', as the building became known after 1884, was built to the designs of Richard Ingram from Southwell at a cost of £15,000. Initially it catered for a mixture of twelve paying and rate–aided patients, but it rapidly expanded in size and capacity. By 1852, when the new St. John's hospital was built at Bracebridge Heath, the Lawn housed a total of 145 resident patients, plus staff. The hospital closed in the mid 1980s and now houses a range of facilities managed by Lincoln City Council.

The Lawn complex, on Union Road in Lincoln, includes an archaeological display centre and the Joseph Banks Conservatory.

The stump of Dunston Pillar stands just off the A15, 10 km (6 miles) south of Lincoln. It is on the route of a public footpath.

The bust of King George III, now in Lincoln Castle grounds, once stood on Dunston Pillar.

DUNSTON PILLAR

Dunston Pillar was erected by Sir Francis Dashwood (of Hellfire Club fame) in 1751 as a land lighthouse to guide travellers across the desolate expanse of heath. It is probably Britain's only land lighthouse. As built, the pillar was 30 metres high, surmounted by an octagonal lantern. Inscribed on its sides, but now barely readable, are the distances to Lincoln and London and a dedication to Dashwood. Around the base he created pleasure gardens with pavilions and a bowling green and the pillar became a fashionable meeting place for the local gentry. The lantern was regularly lit until 1788 but enclosure of the heath and the establishment of a better road gradually made the lighthouse redundant. The lantern was used for the last time in 1808 and fell from the pillar during a storm, a year later.

In 1810 the Duke of Buckingham substituted a statue of George III for the lantern, in celebration of the King's Golden Jubilee. During the second world war the statue was removed and the tower cut down to 10 metres to reduce the risk to aircraft from Coleby Heath airfield. The statue was taken to Lincoln Castle where the upper part is on display.

Hilary Healey

The Grantham Canal at Stenwith near Woolsthorpe By Belvoir.

TRANSPORT BY WATER

Until the end of the 18th century, the transport of bulky goods such as coal and corn was difficult. One solution, which worked well until superseded by the railways, was the construction of canals or navigable waterways.

The idea of building a canal to link Grantham to the River Trent at Radcliffe was first proposed in 1792 but met with opposition from Radcliffe landowners and the promoters of a rival (Grantham to Newark) canal. A revised scheme which connected with the Trent at West Bridgford was accepted in 1793. The Grantham Canal opened in 1797 shipping coal, coke, lime and building materials from Nottingham to Grantham and agricultural produce on the return journey.

Traffic on the canal reached its peak in the mid 19th century but declined with the opening of the Nottingham to Grantham railway in 1850. By 1929 trade had almost ceased and the canal was abandoned in 1936. In the late 1960s a Restoration Society was formed and seven miles of the canal are now navigable again with plans to restore the whole system by the year 2000.

TURNPIKE ROADS

Road transport in the Georgian period became slightly more convenient, although still fairly uncomfortable, through increased use of carriages and coaches travelling on better maintained roads.

Until the mid 18th century, the upkeep of highways had largely been the responsibility of the parishes through which they passed, resulting in rough, slow, and sometimes treacherous journeys. In 1751 an act was passed which made it easier for independent Turnpike Trusts to take on the responsibility for road construction and maintenance, funded by loans and tolls paid by travellers.

The Louth to Horncastle turnpike road was opened in 1770, the same year as the Louth Navigation. It had a toll bar at either end, although within ten years that nearest Louth had to be relocated to prevent wily travellers by–passing the collection point. Paying traffic would have included wagons, carriages and stage–coaches; the Royal Mail coach, the military, and Sunday worshippers were allowed to pass through at no charge.

A sharp eye will spot surviving milestones.

Toll Cottage at Hallington on the Horncastle to Louth turnpike.

GEORGIAN CHURCHES

During the 17th century, perhaps because of the disruption of the Civil War, there was a lull in church building. The Georgian period, however, was more settled, and many new churches were built, and old ones refurbished.

In 1734, the Church of All Saints in Gainsborough was noted to be in a poor condition. The architect Francis Smith of Warwick was engaged to rebuild parts of it, and his work can be seen in the aisle walls and chancel. The round headed windows and simple decoration of this Georgian work contrast with the more elaborate style of the late medieval tower.

The classically–styled Church of St. Margaret's, Well, was a brand new building, designed after the model of a Grecian temple. It was constructed in 1733, and deliberately sited as a focal point for Well Vale House, which had just been remodelled for James Bateman.

Unusually, the church faces east, with the altar at the west end, presumably in order to present a pleasing aspect to the House.

St. Margaret's, Well, a classical composition serving both as a place of worship, and as an attractive feature.

The Church of All Saints, Gainsborough, partly rebuilt in the Georgian period.

VICTORIAN ENTERPRISE

Ashley Black

A stone lion guards Harlaxton Manor.

The Victorian period saw a great flowering of industry, investment and confidence in Lincolnshire. Through the efforts of individual entrepreneurs and established companies a network of railways was gradually developed to transport raw materials and finished products to and from the factories of Lincoln, Grantham and Gainsborough, and later the fast-growing steel town of Scunthorpe. Developments in engineering and the manufacture of agricultural machinery enabled firms like Rustons, Clayton and Shuttleworth, Marshalls of Gainsborough and Hornsbys of Grantham (who developed the first 'chain tracked' vehicles from which the military armoured tank eveolved) to prosper. Meanwhile in the countryside, new farms were carefully planned to capitalise on the increasing mechanisation of agriculture. The Lincolnshire Wolds were, however, still pastoral enough to inspire some of the poet Alfred, Lord Tennyson's finest works.

The 19th century was also an age of great social concern; new churches and chapels were built to improve the spiritual and moral health of the population; hospitals and asylums were opened to cater for bodily needs. For the first time elementary education was made available to all children of whatever social class, and nearly all of Lincolnshire's towns and villages can still boast a Victorian primary school.

The Victorians built with a sense of confidence and adventure – even their most workaday buildings were often on a grand scale and adorned with decorative brickwork. This tendency to decorate was perhaps best demonstrated in their own homes; from flamboyant country houses to the charming estate villages, we are lucky to have many survivals from a period which incorporated past traditions, whilst looking forward to a brave new age.

Ashley Black

Harlaxton Manor, a private property which is occasionally open to the public.

VICTORIAN COUNTRY HOUSES

Where Georgian architecture tended to be restrained in its combination of new style and historic features, Victorian architecture shook up the mix and doubled the ingredients, resulting in some elaborate creations.

Harlaxton Manor, near Grantham, is a breath–taking marriage of Elizabethan details and Victorian invention on a massive scale. The house was built for Gregory Gregory de Ligne by the architect Anthony Salvin in the 1830s, while the exterior works and screen were designed by William Burn. The reason for the size and opulence of the house remains a

Part of the sumptuous baroque interior.

Ashley Black

mystery, as Gregory had no heirs to pass it on to, but rumour has it that he was trying to out–do the owners of nearby Belvoir Castle, which was refurbished in 1825.

The house was almost derelict by the 1930s, but was saved by the enterprising Mrs Van der Elst who part–funded the repairs by the sale of her beauty preparations (she developed 'Shavex', the first brushless shaving cream). Harlaxton Manor is now a college of the American University of Evansville.

Travellers on the A155 to Skegness may just glimpse the now ruinous Revesby Abbey, set in its deer park behind ornate entrance gates.

The present house was built in 1844 by William Burn for J. Banks Stanhope, in a style echoing the Elizabethan theme seen at Harlaxton. It replaced an earlier house bought by the Banks family in 1714. Earlier still, Cistercian monks had built an abbey nearby during the 12th century, but their remains had no doubt long disappeared by the time Revesby's most renowned resident, Sir Joseph Banks (1743 – 1820) was in occupation. Sir Joseph is best remembered for

his contribution to botany. He voyaged the world with Captain Cook collecting rare plants and was elected President of the Royal Society in 1778. The decaying arboretum at Revesby still contains some rare specimens which may owe their discovery to Sir Joseph. He was very influential in Lincolnshire, being involved, among other things, with schemes for the Horncastle and Sleaford Navigations.

Revesby Abbey is not currently accessible to the public, but there are long–term plans to restore this once dignified building.

IMPRESSIVE ENTRANCES

For centuries the majestic form of the triumphal arch has been used to celebrate eminent people or significant events. The best known example is probably the *Arc de Triomphe* in Paris. The Brocklesby Memorial Arch and the Lion Gate at Scrivelsby are much smaller structures, but they too are built to commemorate famous people, as well as to create a grand entrance into a country estate.

The Brocklesby Arch, built in 1864 spans the Brigg road at the western entrance to Brocklesby Park. Inscriptions on either side record that it was built as a memorial to the second Earl of Yarborough by his grateful tenants and friends. The gateway to Scrivelsby Court is surmounted by a regal lion, the emblem of the Sovereign's Champion. This office has been held by the Dymokes of Scrivelsby since the 14th century.

The Lion Gate at Scrivelsby.

The Brocklesby Memorial Arch.

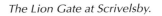

The gateway was erected around 1530 and restored in 1833. The adjacent gatekeeper's lodge was reputedly designed by Humphrey Repton, the landscape gardener who laid out the grounds of the Court in the late 18th century.

HOMES FOR WORKING PEOPLE

A growth in the rural population, plus increased availability of materials such as brick and tiles, prompted a gradual increase and improvement in rural housing during the early 19th century. Lincolnshire still had many overcrowded hovels but amongst them new cottages, villages and terraces were springing up. Many were constructed by speculative builders to a very basic plan, but some were architect designed, although the architect's aesthetic vision did not always match the scale of the location.

Barkham Street, in Wainfleet, is an example of one such mismatch. On his death, local landowner Sir Edmund Barkham made a bequest to the Bethlehem Hospital, London. The Hospital had already built some tenements in Southwark, and in 1847 used the same plans, by Sidney Smirke, to build the terraces in Wainfleet, giving an incongruous result.

Barkham Street in Wainfleet All Saints –
a London street in a quiet country town.

The Tudor style estate cottages of Blankney village, however, sit more harmoniously in their surroundings. The village was designed by W. A. Nicholson in the 1830s, and seems to reflect an idealised vision of the late medieval past.

The picturesque estate village of
Blankney was built for the Chaplin
family, residents of the now
demolished Blankney Hall.

Waddingham village green.

VILLAGE FEATURES

Rural life in Victorian Lincolnshire centred around the village, which was far more self–sufficient than today. What could not be grown or made, could be bought from a wide variety of shops. As well as the expected butchers and bakers, Heckington in 1856 could boast a hat–maker, a tinner, a nailmaker and a cooper.

Many villages were centred around a green, used for fairs, markets and recreation. Nettleham village green had three pairs of stocks, where petty criminals would be secured for public humiliation. Horses, cattle and sheep were watered at village ponds, whilst drinking water came from wells, pumps and streams. The lack of adequate sewers and drains in larger settlements often made such communal supplies dangerous. In 1904, Lincoln's water supply became contaminated, and the resulting typhoid outbreak caused 131 deaths. Safer drinking water was carried in carts from the village of Welton until 1911 when the opening of a new pipeline brought water to the city from Elkesley in Nottinghamshire.

Cast iron water pumps in the shape of a Classical column with a lion's head water spout were made by Glenfield & Co of Kilmarnock in the late 19th century. This one is in Washingborough, but they can be seen in many Lincolnshire villages.

One of two well covers in Coleby.

Relic of a bygone age; a mounting block for horsemen in Caythorpe.

CRIME AND PUNISHMENT

The system of law and order in Victorian Lincolnshire was strict and, it seems, fairly effective. A Parish Constable would deal with minor local crimes, but where there were threats of violence on a larger scale, such as during the Swing Riots (against unemployment caused by the introduction of threshing machines), magistrates organised the swearing–in of additional Special Constables. Penalties were severe; drunkenness or sleeping rough brought a fine or imprisonment whilst several months' hard labour (or before 1853 transportation for repeat offenders) was the reward for stealing small items. At the beginning of the 19th century 200 categories of offence could incur the death penalty. The efforts of reformers like Sir Robert Peel reduced this to fifteen in 1837, and by 1870 the gallows were only used for cases of murder or high treason.

The lock–up in Deeping St. James was converted from a 15th century cross–base, and also served as the village pump. Criminals would be impounded here overnight before being taken to the Police Court in Bourne.

The lock–up in Deeping St. James.

Hilary Healey.

Grantham Barracks was used as a concert venue in the 1950s, and subsequently became part of Grantham College. It is now an antiques showroom.

MILITARY BUILDINGS

In Victorian times the defence of the realm was undertaken at several levels: the regular army, the militia, the volunteers and the yeomanry.

Conscripts to the militia were drawn by ballot from lists of men of working age. Following several years of service, the militiaman could transfer to the regular army. Grantham Barracks was built for the Royal South Lincolnshire Militia in 1858, at a cost of £3640, and was extended to include housing and a hospital in 1872. During the first world war, wounded soldiers were treated here by a Voluntary Aid Detachment.

Lincoln Drill Hall, built for the Volunteers in 1890, was affectionately known as the 'Bread and Cheese Hall' after the nickname of its founder, the industrialist Joseph Ruston, who was irreverently called 'Old Bread and Cheese'. In the 1950s the Hall was used as a venue for concerts given by such luminaries as Ted Heath, the great trombonist. In those days it was known locally as 'The Trap', for once inside, it was very difficult to get out!

The Drill Hall, which still contains its rifle range, is now managed by the City Council, and hosts concerts and events.

93

The 'planned' Manor Farm at Kirmond–le–Mire, a rare and important survival from the days of Victorian high farming.

HIGH FARMING – VICTORIAN STYLE

The increasing demand for food created by a growing population, and the widespread availability of steam–powered machinery were both factors in the mid 19th century trend towards 'high', or industrialised farming.

One of Lincolnshire's foremost agricultural improvers was Christopher Turnor, who used inherited wealth to build a grand new home for himself at Stoke Rochford, and to improve the family farms.

Manor Farm at Kirmond–le–Mire was built by Turnor in 1868 with a layout organised for maximum efficiency. An E-shaped plan incorporates two crew yards surrounded by beast sheds. Here, cattle were fattened, and manure, valuable as a fertilizer, was collected.

Stables, waggon sheds and barn were included in the layout, along with a steam engine which would have driven slicing, cutting and threshing machines. Some of the machinery has survived, including a mill made by the Lincoln firm of Clayton and Shuttleworth, who were recorded as having produced 1200 steam engines and 900 threshing machines in 1870.

THE POWER OF WIND AND WATER

Windmills are a distinctive feature of the Lincolnshire landscape, and in the early Victorian period there were around 500 countywide, used for the production of flour, cereals and animal feeds. Most were brick tower mills, often with a coat of black tar as a precaution against damp. The number of sails varied between four and eight, and they were turned into the wind by a fantail on the opposite side of the wooden cap. The five–sailed Dobson's Mill in Burgh–le–Marsh was built in 1813 by local millwright Oxley of Alford. It is unusual because the sails turn clockwise when viewed from the front – most turned the other way.

The power of water was also harnessed by mills; the great wheel was turned by water hitting it either from axle height (a breast–shot wheel), from below (under–shot), or from above (over–shot). The breast–shot wheel at Ketsby Mill was fed by a stream rising high in the Wolds, and eventually flowing to join the Great Eau.

The last iron waterwheel to turn in the county is found at the privately owned Ketsby watermill, built around 1864.

Dobson's Mill is a working mill, owned and managed by Lincolnshire County Council and open to the public.

LOCAL INDUSTRIES

During the 19th century many manufacturing and processing industries flourished in Lincolnshire. To be efficient, they needed to be close to both the source of raw materials, and a transport link for distribution of the finished product.

The brick and tile making works on the banks of the Humber had both these advantages. They were sited on reserves of high quality clay, which could be used to make pantiles, finials and chimney pots as well as ordinary bricks. The products were exported via the network of inland waterways and the coast to the industrial Midlands, London and East Anglia.

Tileries at Barton on Humber, seen from the Humber Bridge.

In Heckington, the pea sorting warehouse leased by the seed firm of Charles Sharp of Sleaford was built by the Great Northern Railway in 1890, adjacent to the station, which had been opened in 1859. Some 400 acres of peas and beans were grown in the area each year. The peas would be taken into the building, and graded by ranks of local women before being put into sacks and sent on by train.

Heckington Pearoom, built in 1890 and used as a pea sorting warehouse until 1961. The Pearoom was repaired and converted by the Heckington Village Trust, and now houses a heritage and craft centre run by North Kesteven District Council.

FEN DRAINAGE

The process of changing the Lincolnshire Fens from wetland to the productive arable area of today began in the medieval period, but took place largely from the mid 18th to the mid 19th centuries. Previously the Fens had been used as common land; grazing for sheep and cattle and hunting ground for fish and wildfowl. Successive Enclosure and Drainage Acts gradually secured large tracts of land against tidal flooding. Individual fields were marked out and surface water carried away by dykes and drains.

As the waters receded peat shrinkage caused the ground level to sink, until much of it was below sea–level. At first, wind powered pumps did the job that gravity could not, but the development of the steam engine provided a new means of pumping surplus water along the dykes and drains to the sea.

The Pinchbeck Engine was built in 1833, and had a steam powered 6.7 metres diameter wheel fitted with scoops to drain about 4000 acres.

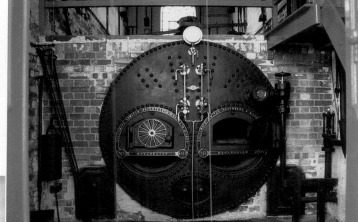

The Pinchbeck Engine was replaced in 1952, and was the last such machine to work in the Fens. It has now been preserved by the Welland and Deeping Internal Drainage Board, and is home to a drainage museum run in partnership with South Holland District Council.

The unusually tall signal box at Kirton was built around 1899, in order that the signalman could see over the adjacent road bridge whilst controlling trains on the Grimsby to Sheffield line.

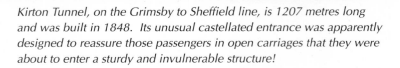

Kirton Tunnel, on the Grimsby to Sheffield line, is 1207 metres long and was built in 1848. Its unusual castellated entrance was apparently designed to reassure those passengers in open carriages that they were about to enter a sturdy and invulnerable structure!

THE AGE OF STEAM

The Victorian period was the great age of the steam railway, and a network of lines was developed across Lincolnshire, linking the towns to the coast, and the county itself to the rest of the country. Most of the lines were run by large companies like the Great Northern Railway, but some were locally owned.

The East Lincolnshire Railway was one of the first to operate in the county, linking Grimsby to Boston via Louth. Unlike some other companies,

it made large investments in the quality of stations such as Louth, built by Weightman and Hadfield in 1848.

Behind many of the railway companies were local entrepreneurs – the Earl of Yarborough was involved in the Great Grimsby and Sheffield Railway which linked the two towns. The line opened in 1849, and is still occasionally used to transport imported coal from Immingham to the Trent Valley power stations.

The charming station at Louth was finally closed to passengers in 1970. It now stands in the middle of a modern estate.

The line from Peterborough to Doncaster was built in 1852 by the Great Northern Railway, and passes over a viaduct which dwarfs the village of Little Bytham. It was along this stretch of line in 1937 that the locomotive 'Mallard', travelling at 126mph, broke the world record for steam traction.

THE VICTORIAN SEASIDE

Pleasure trips to the seaside were unheard of for most people in the early Victorian period, until the coming of the railways, with their cheap day–return tickets to the coast. The line from Grimsby to Cleethorpes was opened in 1863, making this the first accessible resort for city people. Skegness, the planned town laid out by the Earl of Scarbrough, was linked to the railway network in 1873, followed by Mablethorpe in 1877 and Sutton–on–Sea in 1886. Industrial workers would start saving at Christmas for their annual outing; some even pawned their belongings to pay for the ticket. The excursions took place on the same day each year, traditionally known as 'Trips Saturday' after the date chosen by the Lincoln foundry workers. Once at the seaside, the trippers filled their day with walks along the pier, playing skittles or strolling in the Skegness Tower Gardens, and taking donkey rides along the beach before making the song–filled train journey home.

Cleethorpes Pier, opened in 1873 but partly dismantled after the second world war.

In the early 19th century entrepreneur John Parkinson of Old Bolingbroke planned and started to build the township of New Bolingbroke. The church of St. Peter was designed by S.S.Teulon in 1854.

The work of Sir George Gilbert Scott can be seen at St. Paul's, Fulney, near Spalding.

VICTORIAN CHURCHES AND ARCHITECTS

The Victorian age was a prolific time for church building and restoration, and Lincolnshire commissions attracted architects with national reputations.

Sir George Gilbert Scott, designer of the Foreign Office building in London, worked in Lincoln and Spalding. Samuel Sanders Teulon, whose work is often recognisable by his fondness for decorative brick banding, designed, altered or restored around fifteen churches in the county.

Restoration was a controversial subject, with great debate between those who preferred to consolidate the existing fabric including alterations made through time, and those who wanted to take churches back to their 'true' medieval form, reinstating and sometimes inventing 'historic' details.

Notable local church architects included the Sleaford firm of Kirk and Parry, and James Fowler of Louth, a prominent and respected citizen who became Mayor of the Borough in 1874. His commissions included secular buildings, for example the De Aston School in Market Rasen, as well as over 100 schemes for Lincolnshire churches.

NON–CONFORMIST CHAPELS

Non–conformist congregations, freed from religious persecution, grew in numbers during the Victorian period and many new chapels for Methodists and Baptists were built around the county to provide appropriate and comfortable surroundings for worship. With their doctrines of repentance and abstinence, the Methodists were particularly successful in attracting followers from the poorer sections of the population.

The chapels were often built from the proceeds of public appeals and bank loans, and their size and ornamentation reflect the wealth of their congregations. Some are tiny, no bigger than a large garden shed, but their very existence stands as a symbol of the faith and determination of their builders. Others are more substantial, with window tracery in the medieval or classical styles, and often decorated with different coloured bricks. John Wesley, who died in 1791, often preached in Lincolnshire; no doubt he would have been gratified by the high attendances recorded at Methodist Chapels (about half of all those attending worship) when a census was taken one Sunday in 1851.

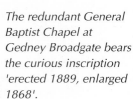

Whaplode Wesleyan Methodist Chapel, built in 1838.

The redundant General Baptist Chapel at Gedney Broadgate bears the curious inscription 'erected 1889, enlarged 1868'.

VICTORIAN SCHOOLS

In order to supplement family income, many Victorian children were sent out to work. In 1867 the passing of the Child Labour Employment Act made it illegal to employ any child under the age of eight but it was not until the Education Act of 1870 that all children were provided with a place at an elementary school. The Education Act created the demand for a wave of new school building in the late 19th century.

The National School in Heckington had been in existence since at least 1843, but was extended in 1873 to provide 80 more places. Attendance varied, as children were needed to help with the harvest, or for special events – perhaps a welcome diversion from the staple diet of reading, writing and arithmetic with the odd geography or history lesson thrown in.

The former National School in Heckington. Replaced by a modern primary school in the late 1980s, it is now the home of the Heritage Trust of Lincolnshire. Some of the staff of the Trust appear in the photograph.

THE TWENTIETH CENTURY

The Lancaster bomber of the Battle of Britain Memorial Flight – a striking symbol of Lincolnshire's role as 'Bomber County' during the second world war.

Throughout history, Lincolnshire has undergone a continuous process of change and development, yet it seems that in no period has the pace of change been so rapid as in the 20th century.

In 1900, Lincolnshire householders drew water from wells for their daily needs, travelled by horse and cart, and learnt about the outside world only through books, newspapers and travellers bearing news. At the close of the century, inter–continental jets pass over us daily and the Internet flashes information around the world at the touch of a button (yet I fear we may soon be drawing our water from wells again!).

This century has seen two world wars, with the county playing a prominent part in the provision of men, machines and facilities. Holiday resorts have sprung up and prospered on the east coast, and the leisure industry has developed to meet the needs of a population with more time and resources to spare than ever before. Industry still thrives in Lincolnshire's towns, and farming has become ever more intensive and automated, leading to the 'prairie' type landscape seen in the Fens.

At the end of the 20th century, Lincolnshire seems to be flourishing. The county combines a respect for its heritage and traditions with an enlightened vision, symbolised for many in the construction of the new University of Lincolnshire.

BASS MALTINGS

In 1905, what was to become one of the county's best known landmarks and a monument to industrial history was opened after a construction period of six years.

The great Sleaford maltings built for the Burton–on–Trent brewing firm of Bass, Ratcliff and Gretton contained eight distinct malting blocks with a central tower housing an engine, workshops and an artesian well 50 metres deep. The whole site was served by its own internal railway, complete with locomotive, connected to the Sleaford to Bourne line. The huge complex, designed by H. A. Couchman, has a frontage of over 300 metres, which is the largest of its kind outside Burton.

The Bass Maltings were closed in 1960, since when the buildings have been occupied by other local firms including the poultry producers, Padleys. A serious fire in 1976 damaged three blocks, but their robust construction ensured that the buildings survived, albeit roofless.

The mighty Bass Maltings in Sleaford were apparently used as a landmark by the Luftwaffe during the second world war.

AGRICULTURE AND HORTICULTURE

Lincolnshire's fertile soil has ensured that during the 20th century, agriculture has remained the major industry of the county. Many acres, especially in the Wolds, are given over to arable farming; a high proportion of root and vegetable crops (the county supplies 35% of the nation's onions) are grown in the Fens. Intensive poultry production units flourish, but flocks of sheep and herds of cattle are something of a rarity.

The horticultural industry has flourished in the Fens, producing acres of colourful flowers. The industry began in the 1880s with the growth and sale of snowdrops, and developed with the large scale production of daffodils for the London market in the 1900s. The introduction of the Darwin Tulip to the county by Samuel Culpin in 1905 added diversity to the industry, and special trains were chartered to provide fast transport

for the delicate produce. In the 1930s special trains also bought thousands of day trippers, eager to see the spectacle of Spalding's bulb fields.

Harvesting in the Wolds.

The beds of tulips were traditionally six rows wide with the seventh row for access. The industry provided employment for many local women. Recently fewer tulips have been grown, but glowing yellow daffodil fields can still be seen.

PARTNEY SHEEP FAIR

Each year, thousands of motorists bound for the Lincolnshire coast pass through Partney, few realising that this quiet village was the site of one of our busiest and most ancient markets. There was a market here before the Domesday Survey of 1086, one of only seven listed in the county. A Royal Charter for a Saturday market was received some time in the 13th or early 14th century, but Partney's importance had already been overshadowed by nearby Spilsby market.

Despite this new competition, Partney market appears to have survived into the early 17th century, a time when many declining markets were replaced by annual fairs. Partney had three annual fairs, primarily dealing in sheep and cattle, held on the 1st and 25th of August and the 18th and 19th of September. One of these – the Partney sheep fair – is still held on 1st August and now specialises in rare breeds.

There were once many annual fairs held in Lincolnshire towns and villages. Partney sheep fair, held on 1st August, is one of the few to survive.

A few early cast iron signposts survive around the county, although they are fast being replaced by their modern counterparts.

ROAD TRANSPORT

If the Victorian period was the great era of the railway, then it is the motor vehicle that has provided the most popular form of transport for people and goods in 20th century Lincolnshire.

A new type of road surface had been pioneered in the 1820s by John McAdam, and in the 1870s the road maintenance responsibilities of the turnpike trusts were taken over by new highway districts. The improved roads would have softened the ride somewhat for passengers in the first solid–tyred 'horseless carriages' which appeared in the 1900s. Although speedometers did not become obligatory until 1927, there was a general 20mph speed limit enforced from 1903 to 1930. There was some antagonism towards the new motor cars, and local police were particularly enthusiastic in their pursuit of speeding offenders. In a defensive move of 1905, the Automobile Association was formed, initially to organise a network of patrols which would warn motorists of impending speed traps. The AA was also responsible for signposting roads until the early 1930s.

The remains of an early petrol filling station still stand on the A155 near Mareham le Fen. The pumps are now used by farm vehicles.

The Tor Anglia leaving Immingham Dock.

IMMINGHAM DOCK

Lincolnshire's medieval prosperity was built on the maritime trade of its coastal ports sited on river havens. Natural processes caused silting of the river channels which, coupled with the growing size of seagoing ships, led to the decline of trade and of Lincolnshire's commercial fortunes.

Immingham was a small port in medieval times but by the 15th century its channel had silted up

and trade dwindled. In 1901 the Great Central Railway obtained permission to build a new dock at Grimsby, but the lack of sufficient depth of water there caused the site to be shifted to Immingham where the deep water channel of the Humber is closest to the south bank. Six million tons of earth were shifted to create a 45 acre dock basin linked to the Humber via a massive lock. Immingham dock opened in 1912 with the capacity to load 5000 tons of coal an

hour from its seven coal hoists served by 272 km (170 miles) of railway sidings. Today, coal isno longer exported but the dock has retained its importance as a major port. Immingham now handles cargoes of dry and liquid bulk commodities, many of which are products of the petrochemical industry which has grown up around Immingham since the 1950s.

Cottam Power Station, on the Nottinghamshire side of the River Trent, began work in 1968 and uses 58 million cubic metres of river water a year, a large proportion of which is returned after use. This huge plant, which generates electricity for the National Grid, is owned by PowerGen.

RIVERS AND INDUSTRY

Rivers provide both a means of transport and a convenient source of water. Because of this, industries have often been established along their banks. In 1842 Nathaniel Clayton and Joseph Shuttleworth set up a small engineering works on a 1¼ acre site by Stamp End Lock on the Witham Navigation. The waterway was used for the transport of raw materials and goods, and at one time a branch extended into the heart of the plant. The firm of Clayton and Shuttleworth flourished in the first quarter of this century, and built the nearby Titanic works (so named as it had the same dimensions as the ill–fated liner) in 1912.

Stamp End Lock is still used by pleasure craft in the 20th century, and the old Clayton and Shuttleworth building is now partially occupied by the Starglaze Group.

Gravel barges can still occasionally be seen on the River Trent, which flows from North Staffordshire to the Humber, but the majority of boats are now pleasure craft. The Trent provides water for the three power stations between Newark and Gainsborough, and is noted for its tidal wave known as the Eagre, which can be seen as far inland as Gainsborough.

The memorial to 617 Squadron (the Dambusters) at Woodhall Spa is in the shape of a dam.

LINCOLNSHIRE AT WAR

Lincolnshire played an important offensive and defensive role in two world wars. Although its easterly coastal position made the county vulnerable to attack from sea and air, its topography ideally suited the establishment of airfields. Twenty were built here in the first world war and 46 in the second.

Among many heroic RAF operations, the raid on the Ruhr dams on 16th May 1943 is one of the best remembered. Nineteen Lancasters of 617 Squadron (the Dambusters), led by Guy Gibson, attacked three dams using the 'bouncing bombs' designed by Barnes Wallis. Two of the dams were destroyed, but at a cost of 53 aircrew and eight aircraft. The memorial to the Dambusters, in the shape of a dam, is at Woodhall Spa, the home of 617 Squadron at the time of the raid.

A hexagonal concrete pill box on the dunes at Gibraltar Point.

Seaborne invasion was considered to be a very real threat in 1940. The Lincolnshire coast was taken over by the armed forces and a wide range of defensive structures built. Concrete pill boxes, some disguised as sheep pens or beach chalets, appeared on the dunes and at strategic points on railways and roads. Lines of four foot concrete cubes were laid out on the beaches as anti-tank defences and miles of barbed wire were strung along the sandhills to impede invasion forces. Remnants of these installations still survive in many places, especially along the coast.

NX611, an Avro Lancaster B MkVII, is the centrepiece of the display at the Lincolnshire Aviation Heritage Centre at East Kirkby.

BOMBER COUNTY

Fifty five years ago thousands of visitors came to this county, not by choice, but by order, posted to one of the 46 RAF and USAAF airfields that were to earn Lincolnshire the name 'Bomber County'. To this day the Avro Lancaster Bomber remains a symbol of Lincolnshire during those grim days. This remarkable aircraft was introduced in 1941 and over 7000 were built before the Lincoln replaced it in 1946.

There are two Lancasters still in Lincolnshire:

PA474 is one of only two in the world still flying, as part of the Battle of Britain Memorial Flight based at RAF Coningsby; NX611 is on display at the Lincolnshire Aviation Heritage Centre at East Kirkby.

Lancaster NX611, built in April 1945, was sold to the French Naval Air Arm in 1952 and saw service in Morocco and New Caledonia before being withdrawn in 1964. It was acquired by the Historic Aircraft Preservation Society who

brought it back to England in 1965. In 1973 NX611 was moved, by road, to RAF Scampton where it was refurbished and became the 'Gate Guardian' of the camp for the next fourteen years. It was transferred to its present home, to become the centrepiece of the Lincolnshire Aviation Heritage Centre, in 1988. Restoration work continues to bring NX611 back to flying condition.

MILITARY COMMUNICATIONS

Communications are a vital factor in any defensive system, and Lincolnshire, 'home of the RAF', has a site unique in the history of aviation communications at Stenigot.

The Chain Home Radar Site was one of twenty original stations in the world's first air defence radar system, and started work in 1939. It is now disused, but has the most complete transmitter mast to survive in an original location. Associated buildings surround the transmitter mast, but the most eye–catching structures on the site come from another communication system; ACE HIGH. The four great 'dishes', two pointing south to Kent and the others pointing to Northumberland, were part of a system which carried air defence radar data and communications between NATO sites in a network stretching from Norway to Greece. The system was built around 1960, and used tropospheric scatter to radiate and receive radio energy over long distances, before it was taken out of service in 1992.

The ACE HIGH dishes at Stenigot are visible from many points of the surrounding Wolds.

TWENTIETH CENTURY HOUSING

Today, basic home amenities such as mains water, gas, electricity and sewerage are taken for granted, but only during this century has this general improvement in living conditions come about.

Part of the credit is due to local authorities, who, prompted by government legislation like the 1919 Housing Act, built large numbers of rented 'homes fit for heroes' (with modern conveniences) during the inter and post–war periods. The development of town planning, and the popularity of 'garden suburb' type schemes led to the construction of spacious new estates (such as Lincoln's Swanpool), with large gardens and tree–lined roads, on land newly allocated for housing. As an alternative to renting, the increasing availability of mortgages in the 1930s encouraged people to buy their own homes. The demand for new houses was often met by speculative builders, who, using the popular mock Tudor and 'arts and crafts' styles, lined the approach roads and outskirts of towns with the villas and semi–detached houses, so different from the late Victorian terraces, and familiar to us today as 'suburbia'.

Original 1930s 'suntrap' windows, so called because they were designed to let as much sunlight into the house as possible. The same principle is used in the style of the large rectangular windows of Shillaker Court in Bourne.

The County Offices, Lincoln. From here, the County Council manages Lincolnshire's schools, social services, libraries, police and fire services, highways and many other services, with a budget of just over half–a–billion pounds in 1994/5.

THE COUNTY OFFICES, LINCOLN

Few people, looking at the extensive offices of Lincolnshire County Council on Newland, Lincoln, would realise that at the core of the complex is a late 18th century house. When the offices were built, in the early 1930s, Lincolnshire was divided into three administrative areas: Holland, Kesteven and Lindsey. The latter included Lincoln, which then, as now, also had its own separate urban authority. Thus the city was the natural home for the headquarters of Lindsey County Council, designed around a courtyard in a Neo–Georgian style by County Architect, H. E. Gamble. In 1974, the recommendations of the Royal Commission on Local Government in England were followed, and the three areas were united under the administration of Lincolnshire County Council. The Lindsey County Offices became the headquarters of the new County Council.

In the 1974 reorganisation the northern part of Lindsey was taken from Lincolnshire and incorporated into the new county of Humberside. This did not prove popular with resident 'yellow–bellies', and on 1st April 1996 the historic county was re–united, in name at least, with the creation of the two new unitary authorities of North and North East Lincolnshire.

A CONSTANT SUPPLY OF WATER

A reliable supply of fresh water is a modern convenience often taken for granted, but the transition from village pump to kitchen tap has taken place mainly in this century, with significant changes in organisation in recent years.

Until the 1960s most water undertakings were run by District Councils. In 1974 the regional water boards were established, and in 1989 they were privatised.

Evedon Water Tower was built in 1915 by Sleaford Rural District Council. It became redundant in the 1960s, and in 1989 was extended and converted to form a private house to a design by architect Tim Benton.

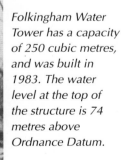

Folkingham Water Tower has a capacity of 250 cubic metres, and was built in 1983. The water level at the top of the structure is 74 metres above Ordnance Datum.

In a relatively flat county like Lincolnshire perhaps the most noticeable symbols of the water industry are the water towers, which began to be constructed in the Victorian period, often to the same design as railway towers.

Water towers are used as an alternative to reservoirs, and provide short term storage with an even pressure through times of peak demand. The hill–top Folkingham tower is filled on a 24 hour cycle, taking water mainly at night from the Southern Lincolnshire limestone aquifer through Billingborough pumping station. The force of gravity then ensures a regular flow to Folkingham and surrounding villages throughout the day.

The Ritz cinema in Lincoln, recently restored to its full neon glory.

THE CINEMA

Britain's earliest recorded piece of film was shot by Birt Acres at the 1895 Epsom Derby. The progress of cinematic technology was rapid, and within a few decades the cinema was one of the nation's main sources of news and entertainment. By 1937, Lincolnshire had 54 'picture palaces', but today only a handful of these once ultra–modern buildings have survived.

Some are still operational; indeed the Ritz in Lincoln, built in 1937 to seat 1600 people, has recently been restored to its full neon glory with the aid of an English Heritage grant. Others have survived through adaptation. Louth and Sleaford cinemas are now partially used as a bingo hall and a snooker club respectively. Still others, like the disused Haven cinema in Boston, are trapped in a perilous balance between demolition for development or retention as historic buildings representative of their period and worthy of protection.

The Kinema in the Woods, at Woodhall Spa, was originally a sports pavilion but was converted to a cinema in 1922. Films are still shown using the rare and original rear projection unit.

THE LINCOLNSHIRE SEASIDE

In 1994, the annual turnover of the Lincolnshire Coast tourism industry was around £214 million, and about $2^1/_2$ million day trippers made their way to towns like Skegness and Mablethorpe, which in 1875 were small villages with populations of 500 and 160 respectively.

The development of Skegness was begun by the Earl of Scarbrough in the 1870s, and continued in the 1920s when Skegness Council opened their newly–built boating lake and swimming pool. The Orchestra Piazza (now the Embassy Ballroom) was opened in 1929, followed by the Sun Castle, or solarium, in 1932. From 1923, annual motor races were held on the broad sands and, staying with the motoring theme, Billy Butlin's Dodgem Track, the first in the country, was opened in 1928. Butlin also opened a 'Luxury Holiday Camp' in Ingoldmells, which offered full board and all–weather entertainment for just £3 a week. It was a new concept, and was to be the first of many such camps, which are now almost a national institution.

The 'bracing climate' of Skegness, immortalised by the Great Northern Railway's Jolly Fisherman poster of 1908, makes these shelters a welcome addition to the promenade in Skegness.

Municipal beach chalets at Sutton–on–Sea.

JOHN WOODWARD'S FANTASY

At the close of the twentieth century it is possible, with the help of computers and the latest machinery, to create structures which only a hundred years ago would have been seen as impossible dreams. 'The Magical World of Fantasy Island' in Ingoldmells is one of the county's newest and most unusual building projects. Opened to the public in May 1995, it is the brainchild of John Woodward, a local businessman who travelled the world to gather ideas. At the heart of this $13\frac{1}{2}$ acre multi level themed attraction is a giant pyramid, which was prefabricated and lifted into place as one piece in February 1995. The crane which was used is one of only two in the world, and is so large that it took 47 vehicles to bring it across the county. Inside the pyramid, fantasy and technology combine to create a 'lost Caribbean Island' complete with lagoon, mountain range and computer controlled hot air balloons.

Whatever will the archaeologists of the next millennium make of this?

Fantasy Island at Ingoldmells, opened in May 1995, has a giant pyramid at the centre of its $13\frac{1}{2}$ acre site which offers Lincolnshire's only indoor hot air balloon experience. It welcomed 3 million visitors in its first season.

THE UNIVERSITY OF LINCOLNSHIRE

Throughout this book, we have celebrated the legacy of previous generations of Lincolnshire inhabitants. To end the chapter on the 20th century, it seems fitting to choose a building project which has been widely recognised as this generation's contribution to the development of Lincolnshire in the next millennium.

The University of Lincolnshire is, at the time of writing, still being constructed on the banks of the Brayford Pool in Lincoln. Planning began in 1993, when a Project Company was set up to mastermind this ambitious and exciting enterprise. The University is scheduled to open in September 1996, when courses on offer will include Criminology, Law, Economics and Tourism. In addition to becoming a centre of academic excellence, the University is expected to have a positive effect on the cultural life of the city.

The University of Lincolnshire; looking forward to the next millennium.

FURTHER READING

There is much published material on Lincolnshire's history and archaeology, less on its architecture. Some of the books are not so easy to find and some are now out of print, however, all of them are available through your local library.

First and foremost must be the Lincolnshire volume of *The Buildings of England* by Pevsner, Harris and Antram, (Penguin Books, 1989). This must be the ultimate handbook for anyone looking at the county's historic buildings but it is a fairly technical book and, despite an extensive glossary, can sometimes be hard to understand. Terence Leach's series *Lincolnshire Country Houses and their Families* (Society for Lincolnshire History and Archaeology 1990, 1993) gives greater detail on some specific buildings. In addition, most of the ancient monuments and country houses open to the public produce their own handbooks and guides as do many churches.

For a systematic study of Lincolnshire's archaeology and history, the ten volumes (twelve are planned) in the *History of Lincolnshire* series are indispensable, although some are becoming a little outdated. They are published by the History of Lincolnshire Committee. Also of interest are *A History of Lincolnshire* by Alan Rogers (Phillimore, 1985) and *Portrait of Lincolnshire* by Michael Lloyd (Robert Hale, 1983). Among the more recent books on the county is the excellent *Historical Atlas of Lincolnshire* edited by Stewart Bennett and Nicholas Bennett (University of Hull Press, 1993). The newly published *North Lincolnshire: A Pictorial History* by Kevin Leahy and David Williams (Hutton Press & N. Lincs. Council, 1996), includes a pictorial review of the archaeology of the Scunthorpe area, with several illustrations of the extraordinary finds from Flixborough.

There are several books examining specific towns in Lincolnshire. For Lincoln itself, Michael Jones' recently published *Lincoln: History and Guide* (Alan Sutton, 1993) is an excellent and very readable guide to the city. Less readily available, but well worth the hunt is *Lincoln – 21 Centuries of Living History* (Lincoln Archaeological Trust, 1984). Although now a little out of date, it is one of the most attractive books to be produced on the history of Lincoln. There is a series of books on Lincolnshire towns published by Barracuda in 'The Book of ....' series, including Boston, Gainsborough, Grantham, Lincoln and Louth. The latest in this series, *The Book of Sleaford* by Simon Pawley has just appeared (Baron Birch, 1996). Stamford is ably described in *The Story of Stamford*, written and published by Martin Smith (Smith, 1994) and information on

Spalding can found in Bernard Clark's *Spalding – the Evolution of a Fenland Town*, (Holland Teachers' Centre, 1978). For Bourne we turned to *The History of Bourne* by J D Birbeck (Warners, 1970).

The development of the coastline and the growth of the holiday industry is admirably dealt with in *The Book of the Lincolnshire Seaside* by David Robinson (Barracuda, 1981). Recent archaeological survey on the Lincolnshire Marshes and the Ancholme valley is included in *Wetland Heritage* by Robert Van de Noort and Paul Davies, (University of Hull 1993). For industrial archaeology we recommend two books: *A Guide to the Industrial Archaeology of Lincolnshire, including South Humberside* by Neil Wright (Society for Lincolnshire History and Archaeology, 1983) and *Civil Engineering Heritage: Eastern Central England* edited by E A Labrum (Institute of Civil Engineers, 1994). The history of the RAF in Lincolnshire and details of past and present airfields are examined in *Bomber County* and *Bomber County 2* by Terry Hancock (Lincolnshire Library Service, 1978 & 1985). A valuable source of information for all aspects of the county is the magazine *Lincolnshire Life*. The Lincolnshire Library Service produces a complete index to all the articles therein, making information very much easier to find.

In compiling **Lincolnshire's Heritage** we consulted very many books, booklets and leaflets, many produced locally by village history groups, heritage bodies, local councils, commercial organisations and individuals. We used many more published sources than those given above but we hope you will find this summary useful. Some of the sources mentioned may be hard to locate, especially those produced in limited numbers or out of print. One of the first stops in any investigation must be the Local Studies section of your library. Their collections are extensive, but more importantly, their specialist staff, who we have always found most helpful, can help pinpoint relevant sources for you and save many hours of searching. For the more determined researcher, Lincolnshire holds one of the best document archives in the country at the Lincolnshire Archives Office ... do not be daunted by the thought of using the county archives; as long as you know what you want, their skilled staff will guide you through. For the widest range of Lincolnshire publications on sale, visit the local history bookshop run by the Society for Lincolnshire History and Archaeology, situated at Jews Court, on Steep Hill, Lincoln. The shop is open Tuesday to Saturday, 10.00am–4.00pm.

PHOTOGRAPHIC CREDITS

Most of the photographs have been taken specifically for this book by the authors and Philip Crome. Particular thanks are due to Philip for his dogged persistence in the face of bad weather, parked cars, scaffolding and telegraph poles. In some cases he has set off with his camera at 4.00am in order to catch a particularly difficult subject, and whilst we have no hard evidence that he has demolished obstructive telegraph poles, there are one or two instances where it seems likely!

Some photographs, particularly those of archaeological objects, have been obtained from the relevant museums and we are most grateful for the assistance of their staff in locating the required photographs. In particular we would thank Tony Page and Kathy Holland of City and County Museum, Mary Powell, the Tourism and Marketing Officer for Lincolnshire County Council, Kevin Leahy of Scunthorpe Museum and Julien Parsons of Sheffield Museum.

We are indebted to the following people and organisations for permission to use their photographs in this book:

Ashley Black:
> Harlaxton Lion (p85)
> Exterior of Harlaxton Manor (p86)
> Interior of Harlaxton Manor (p86)

The British Museum:
> The Witham Shield (p20)
> The Fiskerton Pins (p31)

Chris Cruickshank:
> The Manwarings, Swineshead (AP) (p44)
> Ridge and Furrow at South Reston (AP) (p57)

Ian George:
> The Jews House (p42)

Hilary Healey:
> Grantham Canal at Stenwith (p82)
> Deeping St. James Lock–up (p92)

Kevin Leahy:
> Viking Metalwork (p37)

Lincolnshire County Council, Archaeology Collection:
> Brayford Pool (p10)
> Sudbrook Torc (p16)
> Revesby Beaker (p18)
> Dunston Urn (p18)
> The Charioteer (P21)
> Duck Brooch (p22)
> Exchequergate Mosaic (p27)
> Gaius Valerius Tombstone (p28)
> Saxon Brooch (p29)
> Welton Beads (p36)
> Viking Stud (p43)

Lincolnshire County Council, Conservation Laboratory:
> The Dowsby Incense Cup (p14)

Lincolnshire County Council, Grantham Museum:
> Ancaster Goddesses (p28)

Sheffield Arts and Museums Department:
> Fiskerton Sword (p36)

David Stocker:
> Kirkstead Abbey (p53)
> Tower on the Moor (p59)

David Vale:
> Artist's Impression of Newport Arch (p23)

Publication of **Lincolnshire's Heritage** has been facilitated by the generosity of the many organisations and individuals who have subscribed to, or sponsored the book. Our grateful thanks go to all of those listed below.

SPONSORS

With special thanks to:

LINCOLNSHIRE COUNTY COUNCIL

Lincolnshire County Council and Lincolnshire County Council Libraries

Department of Archaeology, University of Nottingham

Badley Ashton & Associates, Winceby

Jeanne & Bob Bates, Grimsby

BBC Radio Lincolnshire

M. B. Bell

Mr & Mrs R. E. S. Bowser, Hareby, Spilsby

Mr C. E. Brackenbury, Geneva, Switzerland

John Byford & Jane Davis, Skegness

Anne Coltman

Dr R. M. Couch, Little Sutton

Miss S. M. Curtis, Lincoln

David & Joan Gilbert & Family, Billinghay Fen

Mr & Mrs T. Hardy, Lincoln

Mr & Mrs G. W. Hart, Burgh–le–Marsh

Val Hinkins, Cherry Willingham

Brian Clifford Howe, Louth

Richard Leary, Spilsby

Louth Naturalists' Antiquarian & Literary Society

Keith & Pauline Loven, Loven & Co

Peter & Phyl Montgomery, Scothern, Lincoln

Miss E. E. Norris, Nettleham

G. R. Prentice, Sleaford

Mr R. R. Read, Binbrook Motors

E. & M. Richardson, East Keal

Malcolm & Jennifer Swire, Boston

Gill Taylor, Friskney

Mrs S. M. Taylor

Joan & Hugh Tilney–Bassett

SUBSCRIBERS

Pamela & John Adams, Alford

R. K. Allday, Boston

David & Shirley Allen, Pinchbeck

A. M. P., Navenby

M. W. A. Andrews, Market Rasen

Mrs Helen Ash, Bassingham

W. A. Ash, Yaxley

L. & A. E. Astbury

Alfred John Atkinson, Flixborough Stather

Revd. Bill Baker, Sutton–on–Sea

Leo Bamber, Bedford

Elizabeth A. Barrick, Lincoln

George C. Bason, Bembridge, Isle of Wight

Eileen Baxter, Grantham

Mrs Audrey Bayles, Woodhall Spa

Michael & Pamela Berry, Middlemarsh

Andy Betts, Lincoln

Neville & Maureen Birch, S.L.H.A., Lincoln

J. P. Bird, Boston

D. G. Boulton, Kirkby on Bain

Mrs Jean Bowes, Long Bennington

Andrew Bramley, Bardney

Mr & Mrs C. E. Bray, Cherry Willingham

A. J. Brooks, Grimsby

Mr & Mrs Michael Brotherton, Wrangle

Mr & Mrs Philip Brown, Frieston

Brenda Butters, Grantham

Rodney & Janet Callow, Lincoln

Barnie Canter, Hallington

Miss E. M. Chester, Spalding

Basil & Pamela Clark, Washingborough

Brett Collier, President, Ramblers' Association, Lincolnshire

Miss Barbara Cook, Boston

George V. Cooke, Riseholme, Lincoln

William & Mary Dales, Mablethorpe

Mike Darwen, Lincoln

A. G. & O. D. Davies, Skegness W.E.A.

Sally, Tudor, Katie & David Dawkins, Heckington

Geoff Dawson, Boston

Anthony John Dent, North Hykeham

R. E. Dickinson, Chippenham

Mr & Mrs G. E. Dixon, Barrow on Humber

Ben Duncan, Ben Duncan Research, Tattershall

Brian Ebb, Grantham

D. J. Edis, Ludford

Marion & Dave Ellis, Braceby

Helen Fenning, Boston

Mr M. A. Ferrier, Louth

Elizabeth Fielding, Boston

Mrs Margaret Forbes, Kuwait

Robin A. Foster, Waltham, Grimsby

Freiston Hall Field Centre, Boston

Mr & Mrs D. George, Cleethorpes

Christopher Godfrey, Cawthorpe, Bourne

Cllr Mike Golding B.E.M., Saxilby

Olive L. Grosvenor, Haxey

Mr & Mrs H. Hackney & Family, Belton

Geoffrey W. H. Hadfield B.E.M., Alford

Sally Hall, Friskney

Hallward Library, University of Nottingham

G. Hardwick, Holton cum Beckering

Richard & Linda Hardwick, Louth

Ernest & Avice Harris, Aubourn, Lincoln

Jean M. Harrison, Skegness

Hilary Healey

Richard & Kay Heath, Pinchbeck

Mrs Pauline M. Hemingray, Middlesbrough

Heritage Studies, Bishop Grosseteste College

Mrs E. I. Heys, Holmes Chapel

D. W. Heywood & P. M. Heywood, Spalding

David & Jean Hill, Woodhall Spa

Canon Peter Hill, Holbeach

Douglas C. Hoare, Sleaford

Ken & Lesley Hollamby, Newburgh, Aberdeenshire

Richard Hollingsworth, Bottesford, Scunthorpe, N. Lincs

Joan Hollingworth, Grimsby

Barbara & Derick Hopkins, formerly of Grimsby

John Honnor, Saracens Head

Geoff Horstwood, Butterwick

Mr Robert Hoyes, Stixwould

A. G. Humphries, Harmston

John Hurst, Stamford

John & Elizabeth Ingleton, Skellingthorpe, Lincoln

Mr T. A. M. & Mrs E. H. Jack

David Jackson, Adelaide, South Australia

E. & H. C. Jackson, Lincoln

Francis Jaekel O.B.E., Woodhall Spa

Richard & Stacey Jefferson, Bourne

Ron & Connie Jepson, Lincoln

K. D. Johnson, Lincoln

M. Jordan, East Barkwith

Mr & Mrs P. Karchewski, Horncastle

John M. Keily, Alvingham, Louth

Gaynor Kirkby, Beesby

Wendy & Bryan Kitson, Epworth

Mr & Mrs C. J. Lester, Branston

Lincolnshire Archives

C. A. Lingard, Billingborough

Michael Lond, Ludford

Mrs P. & Mr L. Lyon, Scunthorpe

Nancy & Roy Malt, Skegness

Mrs A. Marshall, Boston

Mrs M. Martin, Holbeach

Mrs Linda Mason, Caistor

Keith D. May, Caythorpe

Alison McCoy, Horncastle

Mick & Margaret Medcalf, Alford

Janet Mellor, Swinderby

Jane & Julian Millington, Tattershall

Susan Mary Moody, Marton, Gainsborough

Peter J. Moore

Alan & Mary Muggleton, Allington Gardens

Miss F. A. Murray, S.L.H.A. Lincoln

Mr & Mrs E. A. Napier, Boston

Stanley John Nicholls, Tetford

Dr Margaret R. Nieke, York

David & Susan Norris, Legbourne, Louth

Arthur & Dorothy Owen, Thimbleby

P. Paddison, Southend on Sea

Zoë Pagis, Huttoft

Simon Pawley, Sleaford

W. M. Peet, Wainfleet

R. J. & C. M. Penhey, Bourne

R. W. & V. A. Phillips, Lincoln

Mr A. B. Porter

Mr G. Porter

Mr J. S. Poulter, Wing, Buckinghamshire

C. T. Prichard, Andrew & Co.

David & Dorothy Purnell, Ruskington

Mr & Mrs K. J. Raby, Sutton–on–Sea

E. A. & M. F. Raven, Grimsby

Dianne Roberts, Cleethorpes

A. R. Robinson, Gainsborough

Mrs J. Savage, Skegness

Eileen Scott, Lincoln

G. J. Scott, Lincoln

Professor Mark Seaward, University of Bradford

J. Keith Shaw, Wragby

Les Sheehan, BBC Radio Lincolnshire

Tricia & Peter Simpson, Metheringham

A. E. Smith, Willoughby, Alford

Derrick & Sheila Smith, Boston

Eric Smith, Billinghay

Sally Smithson, Kirkstead

Mike Sparkes, Thorney

Stewart Squires, North Hykeham

Mr & Mrs C. Start, Wolverhampton

Mr & Mrs M. Start, Fareham, Hants

Mary Sterland, Southwell

P. E. Stevenson, Heckington

David Stocker, Oxford

Margaret R. Stoddart, Belchford

Mr & Mrs E. Sylvester, Boston

Geoff Taylor, Lincoln

John D. Taylor C.B.E., Holbeach

Peter Thackeray

Ian & Frances Thompson, Scunthorpe

Mr & Mrs W. G. Thompson, Ulceby

Philip P. Towell, Boston

David Vale, Lincoln

Mr & Mrs C. J. Vasey, Rotherham

Miss M. J. Vickers, Lea, Gainsborough

Mrs Margaret Vincent, Horncastle

Mrs Jean A. Waite, Waddingham House

Christopher J. Wales, Great Gaddesden

Derrick & Dorothy Wales, Wainfleet St. Mary

Mrs A. J. Walker, Market Rasen

Mr J. M. Walker, Cardiff

Jill Westgarth, Laughterton

Tourism & Arts Officer, West Lindsey District Council

Mrs M. Whaler

Pearl Wheatley

Paul Whitaker, Dunsby

The Revd. John Wickstead, Skegness

Sarah, Mary & Harry Willis, Newark on Trent

INDEX